THE NATIONAL FLAG

Saint
George's
Cross

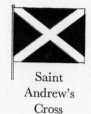

Saint
Andrew's
Cross

Union Jack
or King's
Colors, of 1606

British Red Ensign, or
Merchant Flag
before 1800

Grand Union Flag

The Stars and Stripes

THE NATIONAL FLAG
A History

BY
WILLIS FLETCHER JOHNSON
HONORARY PROFESSOR IN NEW YORK UNIVERSITY

With Illustrations in Color

BOSTON AND NEW YORK
HOUGHTON MIFFLIN COMPANY
The Riverside Press Cambridge
1930

The Riverside Press
CAMBRIDGE · MASSACHUSETTS
PRINTED IN THE U.S.A.

TO
THE DAUGHTERS AND SONS
OF THE
AMERICAN REVOLUTION

PREFACE

TURNING the pages of one of the most comprehensive and authoritative volumes of recent date upon the Flags of the World, in a chapter upon the American Flag I read:

'No flag has received more attention from the orator and romancer . . . and many verse writers have been busy; but producing nothing worthy of their theme; even "The Star-Spangled Banner," sung to its original tune, a piece of music — "Anacreon in Heaven" — composed for the flute, is anything but a masterpiece. A quotation is, however, inevitable, and this will suffice:

> '"When Freedom, from her mountain height,
> Unfurled her standard to the air,
> She tore the azure robe of Night,
> And set the stars of glory there.
> She mingled with its gorgeous dyes
> The milky baldric of the skies,
> And striped its pure celestial white
> With streakings of the morning light:
> Then from his mansion in the sun
> She called her eagle-bearer down
> And gave into his mighty hand
> The symbol of her chosen land."'

Thereupon, after a copious libation to the affronted memories of Francis Scott Key and Joseph Rodman Drake, I ventured to think that if I should write a book about the Stars and Stripes there would be little fear of its containing worse errors than that, while there might be a possibility of its correcting others.

It is true that the correcting of errors seems often an ungracious if not actually an odious performance, especially when the errors exist in long-cherished traditions, strengthened by local pride or ancestral devotion, as is the case with several with which I must deal. Yet a right sense of respect for the National Ensign should certainly cause us, at whatever cost of feeling, to invest it with only 'whatsoever things are true, whatsoever things are honest, whatsoever things are just, whatsoever things are of good report.'

To undertake this work I have been much encouraged — perhaps I might say, inspired — by the more than gracious manner in which, on numerous occasions, some remarks of mine about the Flag have been received by two of the most authoritative and most discriminating of our great patriotic organizations, the Daughters of the American Revolution and the Sons of the American Revolution. To them I shall make bold to dedicate this little book, and their estimate of it will be the best measure of my efficiency in writing it.

WILLIS FLETCHER JOHNSON

SUMMIT, NEW JERSEY
June, 1930

CONTENTS

LIST OF ILLUSTRATIONS

THE NATIONAL FLAG

.· ·.

CHAPTER I

THE COMING OF THE COLORS

THE war was on for American Independence. For more than two years it had been waged under a motley array of flags. Beneath a banner of crimson and silver with the legend 'Conquer or Die!' the 'embattled farmers' at Concord Bridge had 'fired the shot heard round the world.' Beneath the Pine Tree banner the battle of Bunker Hill had been lost and won. Beneath silver crescents on a field of blue Fort Sullivan had resisted the fury of the British fleet. Beneath the Rattlesnake flag and another the first American fleet had won its first victory. Under the 'Meteor Flag of England,' with six white stripes drawn across the crimson field, Washington had captured Boston, rejected Howe's overtures of peace at New York, retreated across New Jersey, turned splendidly at bay at Trenton, and settled securely among the hills at Middle-brook and Morristown. Thenceforward there was to be no thought of compromise, but the campaign was to be fought out defensively but aggressively to a finish.

It was time, therefore, for a new flag to be adopted which should signify something more than any of its predecessors; a flag which should be a token that old things had passed away and that all things had become new in the severance of the last link that bound the Colonies to the Mother Country; a national standard for the United States of America. In such circumstances the Stars and Stripes was born.

The new Flag had, however, a significant ancestry in the various banners of the Colonial era and of the early conflict before protesting insurgence had developed into confident revolution. And its ancestors also had contemporaries and predecessors of other national lineages, upon these shores or near them, during the many years of discovery and exploration and settlement and through the long rivalry for Continental dominance; all of which must have essential place in the prologue of our own Flag's history.

What banners Saint Brendan and other legendary voyagers bore, and whether indeed they actually reached the mainland of this Continent, we may not surely know. But there are those who give much credit to the Islendingabok, and the Landramabok, and the Hauksbok, and the Flateyjarbok, and all the versions of the Sage of Eric the Red; and who therefore reckon that Thorstein and Leif, the sons of Eric, did discover and explore and for a time colonize parts of the coast of North America. If so, they doubtless planted here their flag; a triangular banner, either white or red, bearing the image of a black raven with wings outspread. That was, so far as we have any tangible suggestion, the first European flag on American soil. But its stay here was not lasting and had no permanent results.

The second to approach these shores, and the first of which we have unchallenged and explicit information, did not at once reach the mainland of the Continent, but paused for a time at outlying islands. Yet it was the true pioneer of all that followed and had for a long time an important continental settlement, even in some parts now forming the United States; wherefore we must give it conspicuous place in our story. This was the flag of the united kingdoms of Leon and Castile. Its first and fourth quarters were red, each bearing a golden castle, in token of Castile; and the second and third were white, each bearing in red an heraldic lion, emblematic of Leon. That was the banner which Christopher Columbus bore at the masthead of the Santa Maria and which he planted upon the beach of Guanahani on October 12, 1492. By its side came another, the personal standard of Columbus and the special ensign of his expedition, given to him by the Queen who was his patron. This one hung pendent from a crossbar instead of flying horizontally from a staff, and was of white, bearing in its centre in green a Latin cross, flanked also in green with the letters 'F' and 'Y,' the initials of King Ferdinand and Queen Ysabel, with golden crowns above them. This latter flag was used only by Columbus on his voyages. But that of Leon and Castile was carried by the other early Spanish explorers and conquerors and was thus planted in Florida by Juan Ponce de Leon, and was borne by Hernando de Soto on his famous but fatal march from the Florida coast to the Mississippi River.

The second national flag in North America was that of England, five years after the first coming of Columbus but indeed before the banner of Leon and Castile was planted upon any portion of the mainland; wherefore it may be claimed to have been the first upon the Continent. It was brought hither in 1497 by John Cabot, a Venetian in the employ of Henry VII of England, who visited the coasts of Newfoundland, Labrador, and Canada. This flag was white, with the red Cross of Saint George extended upon it from side to side and from top to bottom — the Crusading banner of Richard the Lion-Hearted. Cabot also bore hither, though not in sovereignty, the Venetian standard, the banner of Saint Mark, scarlet with a broad border of blue and the golden-winged lion of Saint Mark holding in his right paw a cross of gold.

Three years later there followed in Cabot's track the banner of Portugal, borne by Gaspar Corte Real; blue and white, with the royal arms resting upon a globe. It was planted for a time in Newfoundland and probably upon the mainland coast, but no lasting settlements were made beneath it.

The flag of France, then a field of blue with three golden fleurs de lys, probably reached America first in 1524, brought hither by the adventurous Florentine, Giovanni de Verrazano, in the employ of the Father of Letters, King Francis I. He is supposed — though not surely — to have touched at Cape Fear and to have visited the Bay of New York and the New England coast. But that flag certainly came hither, with tremendous effect, in 1534, in the puissant hand of Jacques Cartier, who explored Canada and founded there the empire of New France, comprising for many years much of the present United States.

As the English flag had first been brought hither by a Venetian in English employ, so the flag of the Netherlands was first brought by an Englishman in Netherlandish employ. This was the illustrious Henry Hudson, in 1609, and the banner which he carried at the masthead of the Half Moon up the river which bears his name was that of the Republic of the United Netherlands. It displayed three horizontal stripes of equal width; the uppermost orange, the middle white, and the lowest blue. As it was also the flag of the United East India Company of Amsterdam it bore in the centre of the white stripe the letters V.O.C.A., the initials of the company's name: Vereenigde Oestindische Compagnie, Amsterdam.

Finally, in 1636, the great Chancellor, Oxenstierna, sent hither the Swedish flag, a blue field spanned from top to bottom and from side to side by a golden cross. It was borne by Peter Minuit, the Belgian statesman who had been the chief founder and first Governor of the Netherlandish colony on Manhattan Island; and it flew for some years over the colony of New Sweden, on both sides of the lower reaches of the Delaware River.

Thus at this last-named date five national flags — Spanish, French, English, Netherlandish, and Swedish — were flying in sovereignty over various parts of the continental domain which now knows no banner but the Stars and Stripes.

CHAPTER II

SAINT GEORGE'S CROSS AND UNION JACK

THE five national standards were not destined long to remain sovereign in North America, and it was the fate of that which had come last, and which floated above the smallest colony, to be abolished first. This was the Swedish flag, in the little colony of New Sweden, on the Delaware. One day the sturdy Netherlanders of Manhattan Island and northern New Jersey decided that the Swedes were trespassers on their domain, and that while they might be permitted to remain there, they must subject themselves to Netherlands rule and live under the Netherlands flag. So they sent a military force across the Jerseys and made New Sweden merely an outlying corner of what had at first been New Belgium, but was by this time generally known as the New Netherlands. Thus the number of American flags was reduced to four.

Meantime the flag of the Netherlands had undergone a change of design. The orange stripe at the top had been made red, so that the colors were prophetically red, white, and blue, precisely as in the present flag of Holland; and the letters V.O.C.A. had given place to G.W.C., standing for Geoctroyeerde Westindische Compagnie, as the Dutch West India Company was known in the Netherlands vernacular. It was in 1655 that this flag triumphed over and banished that of Sweden. But in 1664 it in its turn yielded to the *force majeure* that was behind and beneath the King's Colors, and the Dutch colony of New Netherlands was partitioned between the British colonies of New York and New Jersey. For a little time in 1673–74 the Dutch flag was restored, but with that exception the British flag was sovereign until deposed by our Revolution; and the number of flags upon this Continent was reduced to three.

At this time the French flag, which had been changed from a blue to a white field, with golden fleurs de lys, was sovereign over the best part of the Continent. For the French domain in-- cluded all of Canada, and all of the Mississippi Valley from the Allegheny Mountains to the Rockies, and southward al- most to the Gulf of Mexico. Next in extent was the Spanish domain, comprising the Gulf Coast and all the lands west of the Rocky Mountains. The English flag was sovereign over nothing but the coast strip, from Maine to Georgia. Yet it flew over a civilized population ten times as numerous as that of all New France, a people restless, adventurous, and aggres- sive. And it came to pass that at the middle of the Eighteenth Century a young Virginian named George Washington carried the British flag across the mountains into the Ohio Valley, and clashed it in war against the golden lilies of France.

So there came on the Old French War, or French and Indian War, of American history, coupled with the Seven Years' War in Europe; and when it ended another flag had vanished from the North American Continent. The lilies of France bloomed here no more; but the red, white, and blue of Britain prevailed from the Atlantic Coast to the Mississippi River, leaving the extreme South and all at the Far West to the crimson and gold of Spain.

The British flag was seen here in two forms, neither of them being like that of the present time. First came the Cross of Saint George, in the earliest days of exploration; the national flag of England alone. But when England and Scotland were united under James I, there came the King's Colors, a com- bination of the national flags of the two kingdoms; a blue field, bearing the white diagonal Cross or Saltire of Saint Andrew, with the red Cross of Saint George superimposed upon it. That was the first Union flag, to which a hundred and two years later the name of Union Jack was given by Queen Anne. Adopted by royal mandate in April, 1605, it was borne by the expedition which landed at Jamestown in May, 1607, and was thus the first British Colonial flag in America. It was also borne by the Mayflower, probably to- gether with the Saint George's Cross, in 1620, and subse- quently became familiar to all the American Colonies. In

1634, however, the Union flag was strictly reserved for the use of the Royal Navy, merchant ships and land forces carrying only the Cross of Saint George or the Cross of Saint Andrew. But in 1707 Queen Anne prescribed for general use a flag with a red field and the Union Jack in canton, and thus came into existence the familiar British Merchant flag, which is also the Red Ensign of the British Navy, often called the 'Meteor Flag.' Between 1649, when Charles I was deposed and beheaded, and 1660, when Charles II came to the throne, Saint George's Cross was the national flag of England, but the American Colonies largely retained the Union flag, and the Red Ensign prescribed by Queen Anne became their flag down to 1776.

It may be added, though not strictly pertaining to our story, that the Union Jack remained unchanged as the British flag until the Union of Ireland with Great Britain was effected in 1801. Then it was necessary that Ireland should have representation. On the Royal Standard the Harp of Erin could be quartered with the red Lion of Scotland and the 'yellow leopards, strained and lean,' of England. But that was impossible on the Union Jack. So for the latter flag the red diagonal Cross or Saltire of Saint Patrick had to be invented, and placed with its arms parallel with those of the Cross of Saint Andrew. We say it had to be invented, for the reason that Saint Patrick had no characteristic cross. He was not a martyr, as Saint Andrew was, nailed to a cross, but died comfortably in his bed, at a good old age. Yet it seemed not incongruous to place in the flag a red cross called by his name, and indeed to make a red diagonal cross on a white field the national flag of Ireland; though under its own rule the Irish Free State has preferred a flag of another pattern.

A word concerning the Union Jack may also be profitable. The story that the name 'Jack' came from Jacques, the French form of James, because it was adopted by King James I, must be dismissed as apocryphal. As already related, the name was not used, at least officially, until eighty-two years after James's death. There seems to be no question that the flag was thus called when it was carried on the jack-staff, the short upright spar on a ship's bowsprit. Before James I made the Union flag, in the days of Queen Elizabeth, the Cross of Saint George was flown on the jack-staff, and was called the 'Jack' or 'Saint George's Jack.' That definition vindicates the propriety of employing the name 'Union Jack' for the Union or starry canton of the Stars and Stripes when it is similarly used as an independent flag; which of course would be absurd if the phrase were derived from the name of King James.

It should be added, to avoid misapprehension, that while originally the King's Colors and the Union flag or Union Jack were identical, they are now different. The Union Jack is borne by only the vessels of the Royal Navy, and in the cantons of the various ensigns. The King's Colors, made of silk instead of bunting, are borne by the various organizations of the British Army, and consist of the Union flag with a crown and the name of the regiment in the centre.

There can be no doubt that the Colonists for many years before the Revolution were deeply and sincerely attached to the British ensign; and with cause. It had been their flag for generations. Under its folds they had fought half a dozen wars, not only on their own soil but in foreign lands, from Canada to the West Indies. They had won great glory under it, at Louisbourg on Cape Breton, at Havana and Quebec, and on a dozen other fields of battle. So it was but natural that even in insurgency and incipient revolution they should retain it, sometimes with inscriptions or tokens of their own added to its field; and that when the inexorable logic of events compelled its relinquishment, they should retain its hues for their own new flag, and should indeed, as we shall see, make their own flag a direct and acknowledged evolution from its historic design. The red, white, and blue of the Meteor Flag led straight, with a single intervention, to the red, white, and blue of the Stars and Stripes.

CHAPTER III

COLONIAL FLAGS

MANY were the flags of the British Colonies in America, in colors, in designs, and in significance. The British flag itself underwent various modifications, with the assent if not at the instance of the Government; there were special flags for the New England Colonies taken collectively; individual Colonies had their own special flags, just as the States do now; and there were at the beginning of the Revolution special flags for the Navy and for individual military organizations. In 1686 James II through Sir Edmund Andros prescribed for the United New England Colonies the Cross of Saint George with the king's crown and monogram in the centre, but with the rest of Andros's works it was unacceptable. In 1701 the British Government prescribed for them a merchant flag, consisting of a blue field, bearing the Cross of Saint George in broad red stripes extending all the way across it, and the diagonal Cross of Saint Andrew in narrow white stripes, and in the centre a white shield bearing no inscription. Then in 1737 the United Colonies of New England were authorized to use a blue flag, with the red Cross of Saint George in a white canton, and in the upper corner of the canton next the staff a globe representing the world. This flag was also made with a red instead of a blue field, and also, in each color, with a tree instead of a globe in the corner of the canton. Thus this one flag really assumed four different aspects, and of them all that with the red field and the tree in the canton became most popular.

This was the first official appearance of a tree upon the flag, although one seems to have been unofficially used as early as 1704, and marked the beginning of a famous series or group of so-called Pine Tree flags, used especially by the New England Colonies. In fact it was not a pine tree which was depicted upon them, but a fir, or spruce, a tree of a very different shape. But the fir belonged to the pine family, and was like the pine an evergreen, and the botanical distinction between the two was popularly disregarded. A pine tree had been used as an emblem on silver shillings, which were coined in Boston in 1652 from metal seized from Spanish ships, the coins being known as 'pine tree shillings.' Such minting was unauthorized by the Royal Government, and might have been subject to heavy penalty. But when the coins were brought to the attention of Charles II, and he demanded to know what the Colonists meant by making them, the shrewd Colonists explained that they were made in his honor, and that the tree on them was a representation of the great oak in which he had once hidden from his hostile pursuers.

The first Pine Tree banner was that already described, with a blue field and the tree in the canton with the Cross of Saint George; and the second was the same flag with a red field. It is probable that both these were carried by the Americans at Bunker Hill. Benson J. Lossing in his 'Field Book of the Revolution' tells that a lady told him that her father helped to raise the flag at Bunker Hill and it had a blue field; while John Trumbull's historical painting of the battle, which hangs in the Capitol at Washington, portrays it as a red flag. However, as we shall see, historical paintings are not always to be depended upon as accurate authorities. The third Pine Tree banner was blue with a white canton bearing not the Cross of Saint George but merely a green tree in its centre, and the fourth was the same with a red field. The fifth was a white flag with no canton but a big tree, colored green, in the centre of the field. The sixth was a white field with a green tree in the centre, with broad blue stripes along the upper and lower borders, and with the legends 'Liberty Tree' above the tree and 'An Appeal to God' beneath it. Finally, the seventh was a white field with the green tree in the centre, with a rattlesnake coiled about the foot of the tree, and with the legends 'An Appeal to God' at the top and 'Don't Tread on Me!' underneath the snake. On some the legend was 'An Appeal to Heaven.'

This last Pine Tree flag may be regarded as the first of another famous group, known as the Rattlesnake flags; the use of that formidable serpent as an emblem having been suggested by Benjamin Franklin. The second was a yellow field with a coiled snake in the centre, and the third was the same as the second with the addition of the legend 'Don't Tread on Me!' The fourth consisted of thirteen red and white stripes, completely covering the field, with a snake diagonally extended across it and the legend 'Don't Tread on Me!' at the foot; and the fifth was the same as the fourth but with red and blue stripes; while the sixth had red and yellow stripes with the legend at the top. Finally, the seventh was a white field with the snake coiled in the centre, with 'Liberty' at one side of the snake and 'or Death' at the other, and 'Don't Tread on Me!' below it, while at the top was the name of the military organization to which it belonged, 'The Culpepper Minute Men.' Several of these flags, notably the second, fourth, fifth, and sixth, as described above, were much used as the standards of the early Navy. The fourth, with red and white stripes and the snake diagonally extended, is in fact said to have been adopted by the Marine Committee of Congress for that purpose on February 8, 1776, and to have been used by the first Commodore of the Navy, Ezekiel Hopkins.

Another noteworthy banner was adopted in South Carolina at the beginning of the Revolutionary agitation, in defiance of the Stamp Act, and was much used in the war. This was a blue field with no canton, but with a white or silver crescent moon in the place where a canton would be. Sometimes there were three crescents, and sometimes the word 'Liberty' was added, at the bottom. That was the flag which flew over Fort Sullivan, at Charleston, when the British vainly bombarded it, on June 28, 1776, and which was heroically picked up under fire and raised again on a ramrod, by Sergeant William Jasper, when it had been shot from its staff by a British cannon ball. In October, 1779, at Savannah, Jasper repeated that gallant performance, but was fatally wounded while so doing.

Connecticut had a flag bearing the coat of arms of the Colony, with the legend 'Qui Transtulit Sustinet,' and the field was a special color for each regiment — yellow, orange, scarlet, crimson, light blue, dark blue, and white. It was carried at Bunker Hill, and afterward had the legend 'An Appeal to Heaven' added, and thus was used by Massachusetts as well as Connecticut troops.

Rhode Island's banner was designed in 1774 by John Manley, of Massachusetts. It was white, with a blue anchor in the centre and the word 'Hope.' To the same design there was later added a canton containing thirteen blue stars; also a blue canton with white stars; also a blue field with white anchor and white canton with blue stars. There is a question whether the stars were placed in the Rhode Island flag before or after the adoption of the Stars and Stripes in June, 1777. The weight of opinion seems to be that they post-dated that event; yet there are those who hold otherwise and see a direct reference to the Rhode Island flag in the poem printed in the 'Massachusetts Spy' of March 10, 1774, a line of which runs, 'The American ensign now sparkles a star.' The flag of New York, emblematic of its important fur trade, was a white field with a black or dark brown beaver in the centre.

We must also recall the historic flag which was raised at Taunton, Massachusetts, in 1774. This was the familiar red ensign of England, a red field with the Union Jack in the canton, and with the legend 'Liberty and Union' in large letters across the lower part of the field. The significance of this was equivocal, and was a matter of dispute. Most held that it meant liberty for the Colonists under continued union with Great Britain, an interpretation which the use of the Union Jack or King's Colors seemed to confirm, as did also the fact that it was raised by those who called themselves 'American Englishmen.' Yet there were those who insisted that the word 'Union' indicated simply the union of the Colonies in their struggle for liberty. Whichever of these was the true interpretation, the flag was hailed with ardor and enthusiasm by the patriot party, as a symbol of resistance to

British misgovernment and of the increasing determination of the Americans to secure for themselves here the same rights of self-government that their fellow subjects in England enjoyed. It might well, therefore, be regarded as denoting the first stage in the evolution of the Stars and Stripes from the British ensign.

CHAPTER IV

EARLY BATTLE FLAGS

FAMOUS flags were borne in the early years of the Revolution by individual companies, regiments, or brigades, or figured heroically in single conflicts. First of all — and still in cherished existence — was that 'to April's breeze unfurled' at Concord Bridge. This was at that time the flag of the Bedford Minute Men, but it had served many years before as the flag of the Three County Troop in King Philip's War, for which use indeed it was designed and made. It was square in form, and crimson in hue, and upon it, embroidered in silver, were an armor-clad arm and hand grasping a short sword or dagger, three cannon balls emblematic of the Three County Troop, and the legend 'Vince aut Morire' (Conquer or Die). It is of peculiar interest to recall that it was designed and made in England, and that the emblems and words were painted on it with oil colors.

When Washington was chosen by the Continental Congress to be Commander-in-Chief of the American Army, he was escorted from Philadelphia to Cambridge by the Philadelphia Light Horse Troop, an organization of the most aristocratic and gallant young men of that city; which bore a special flag of its own. That flag was nearly square, with a broad border of heavy fringe. Its field was bright and rather light yellow and it had a canton of thirteen blue and silver horizontal stripes. In the centre of the field, in blue and silver, was an elaborate geometrical figure resembling a rosette, surrounded by heraldic emblems, and underneath the legend, on a scroll, 'For These We Strive,' while above were the intertwined initials L H, denoting the Light Horse Troop. It is probable that this flag was carried in the battle of Trenton, since the troop served there, as infantry.

Pennsylvania contributed two other regimental flags which were carried through the war. One of these was crimson,

Pine Tree Flag of
Bunker Hill

Pine Tree Flag of
Early Navy

Virginia Rattlesnake
Flag

Rattlesnake Flag of
Early Navy

South Carolina Flag

Rhode Island Flag

with the Union Jack in canton, and in the centre of the field a coiled rattlesnake and the legend, on a scroll, 'Don't Tread on Me.' There were also the initials, J.P., I.B.W.C.P., which stood for the names of the commander and of the organization — John Preston, 1st Brigade, Westmoreland County, Pennsylvania. The other was the flag of the First Rifle Regiment of Pennsylvania; which had a deep green field, displaying a hunter armed with a spear and a tiger struggling to escape from a trap, the hunter preventing him, with the legend 'Donari Nolo' (I Will Not Yield).

Famous, too, with romantic and sentimental lore, is the Eutaw Standard, the battle flag of Colonel William Washington's troop of horsemen. A Virginian, kinsman of George Washington, that gallant commander was betrothed to the fair Jane Elliott, who lived in the suburbs of Charleston, South Carolina. On the eve of the campaign which led through Eutaw and the Cowpens, he spent an hour with her, and when he said farewell she wished him safety and victory, and said that she would await news of the triumph of his flag.

'But I have no flag,' he replied.

'Then I'll give you one!' she cried; and seizing scissors she cut a square of rich crimson brocade — some say from the back of the cushioned chair in which she had just been seated, while others say it was from a curtain. And that piece of silk, fastened to a tough hickory pole, led the troop through all its daring adventures, and became known throughout the army as 'Tarleton's Terror,' so much trouble did it lead against that ruthless British raider. And when the fighting was done, it was displayed at the wedding of Miss Elliott and Colonel Washington.

The banner of Count Casimir Pulaski is famous in our Revolutionary annals, and has been the theme of poets. When under authority of Congress that Polish patriot organized Pulaski's Legion, of sixty-eight horsemen and two hundred footmen, the Moravian nuns, of Bethlehem, Pennsylvania, made him a flag for it. Poetical legend has it that they did this as a labor of love and of religious devotion, or in gratitude for his protection of their nunnery from molestation. Practical historians more plausibly insist that it was a purely commercial transaction, and that the nuns charged and Pulaski paid a fair price for the banner. However that may be, Pulaski bore the flag gallantly, in more than one fierce fight, and died defending it. It was made of rich crimson silk. On one side were the embroidered letters 'U.S.,' and around them in a circle was the legend 'Unitas Virtus Forcior' (Unity Strengthens Valor). But the good Sisters were at fault in their Latin, misspelling the last word, which should, of course, have been 'Fortior.'

Amid all the variety and sometimes confusion of Colonial flags, the first attempt to establish uniformity was, for obvious reasons, in the embryo Navy. It was indeed necessary that all vessels in the service should carry the same kind of flag, to ensure recognition. So as early as September, 1775, Washington had as adjuncts to the army besieging Boston two floating batteries in the Charles River, flying the white and green Pine Tree flag. Three months later he commissioned half a dozen schooners to cruise in the North Atlantic and intercept British vessels bringing supplies to the British army, the first being the Hancock, under Captain John Manley; and at his recommendation these all flew the same flag. In a letter to Colonel Glover, who was aiding in fitting out the vessels, Washington described it as 'a flag with a white ground and a tree in the middle; the motto, "An Appeal to Heaven."' This flag was further adopted by the government of Massachusetts, in April, 1776, as the flag of the State navy.

Meanwhile, in December, 1775, Congress authorized the creation of a Navy, but did not prescribe a flag for it. So at Philadelphia, under the influence, presumably, of Franklin, the champion of the rattlesnake, the Rattlesnake flag which we have already described was at first adopted. But as another, the Grand Union flag, had been adopted for the Army, when at Christmas-time of 1775 Commodore Hopkins assumed command of the little fleet, both were raised upon his flagship. Apparently the Grand Union flag was raised at the mizzen peak, as the flag of the United Colonies, and the Rattlesnake flag was flown at the main, as the fleet flag, or the Commodore's flag. They were both raised by John Paul Jones, who had been commissioned a First Lieutenant and who was Flag Lieutenant on the flagship of the fleet, and he made it clear in his journal that the Rattlesnake flag was not at all to his liking. 'I could never see,' he wrote, 'how or why a venomous serpent could be the combatant emblem of a brave and honest folk fighting to be free. Of course, I had no choice but to break the pennant as it was given to me. But I always abhorred the device, and was glad when it was discarded for one more appropriate.' Numerous other authentic records of that time confirm the belief that the Grand Union flag was also raised above the vessels, and was in fact regarded as the real flag of the Navy. But we must assume, too, that the Rattlesnake flag was actually carried by Hopkins's fleet on its cruise to the Bahamas, and that under it, as well as under the other, the first triumph of the American Navy was won.

CHAPTER V

THE GRAND UNION FLAG

WE now come to the first national standard of the United States; designed and adopted before the United States itself was formed. There is no record in the Journal of the Continental Congress of any action whatever concerning it. But it is plausibly believed that the flag was decided upon by a committee of the Congress which visited Washington's camp at Cambridge in the fall of 1775. On September 21 of that year Washington wrote to Congress a long letter, with various enclosures, concerning the state of the Army, in response to which, on September 30, Thomas Lynch, Benjamin Franklin, and Benjamin Harrison were appointed a committee 'to repair immediately to the camp at Cambridge, to confer with General Washington . . . and such other persons as to the said committee shall seem proper, touching the most effectual method of continuing, supporting, and regulating a Continental Army.'

This committee returned from its errand on November 1, and the next day made an elaborate report to the Congress, which was considered at length during several days, and led to the adoption of numerous resolutions. These fixed the size of the Army at 20,372 men; provided for the pay, rations, clothing, and arming of the officers and soldiers; and established an elaborate code of rules and regulations. And on November 25 an appropriation of $581.90 was made, to pay all the expenses of the committee on its errand.

The statement has been published in various places that this committee was specially appointed to devise a Continental flag, and that it did so in conference with Washington and some other persons not named, the result being the Grand Union flag. But no authority whatever was given for this statement. Moreover, it was said that the conference with Washington took place at Cambridge on December 13 or 15,

1775, six weeks after the committee had returned to Philadelphia and made its report to Congress. That story may therefore be dismissed as little better than fiction.

There is no mention of the flag in the instructions of the Congress to the committee, or in any of the resolutions adopted by the Congress; so far as these are recorded in the Journal. That does not, however, preclude the possibility of the committee's having discussed the matter with Washington; which indeed there is every reason to suppose that it did, since the adoption of a uniform and appropriate flag for all divisions of the Army was obviously one of the urgent needs of the time. Nor does it indicate that the committee did not report upon the flag to the Congress, or that the Congress did not take some formal action upon it; since the report of the committee is not entered in full or even in synopsis in the Journal, and it is clear that some resolutions were adopted concerning it that are not given in the Journal.

The weight of presumption is, therefore, that the Grand Union flag was devised by Messrs. Lynch, Franklin, and Harrison, in conference with Washingon; and that the Congress acquiesced in their decision. The new flag was at any rate made and hoisted above the vessels of the embryo Navy when Captain Hopkins received his commission and assumed command, the first Commodore of the fleet. There is no reason to suppose that it was raised, however, as early as December 3, when the vessels were first fitted out. The officers did not receive their commissions until December 22, and the flag was probably raised then, or a few days later.

That it was raised by Washington for the first time on January 1 or 2, 1776, on Prospect Hill, Charlestown, and afterward at his headquarters at Cambridge, there is abundant testimony, of the most convincing character. Washington himself wrote to Joseph Reed on January 4 that 'We hoisted the Union flag in compliment to the United Colonies.' On the day of that flag-raising the King's speech, making fruitless overtures to the Colonies, was received, and the British officers and Loyalists in Boston, seeing from afar a flag bearing the

King's Colors in its canton, joyfully jumped to the conclusion that it was a signal of the rebels' surrender! So another letter, written on that very day, but of unknown authorship, said: 'The Grand Union flag of thirteen stripes was raised. The regulars did not understand it; and as the King's speech had just been read, they thought the new flag was a token of submission.' A news letter in Franklin's 'Pennsylvania Gazette,' from Cambridge, reported that 'The Grand Union flag was raised on the 2d, in compliment to the United Colonies.'

The British were soon undeceived, however, concerning the meaning of the new flag. The captain of a British vessel, writing from Boston a fortnight later, said: 'I can see the rebels' camp, very plain, whose colors a little while ago were entirely red; but on the receipt of the King's speech (which they burned), they hoisted the Union flag, which is here supposed to intimate the union of the Provinces.' Again, the 'British Annual Register for 1776,' recorded that 'The arrival of a copy of the King's speech, with an account of the fate of the petition from the Continental Congress, is said to have excited the greatest degree of rage and indignation amongst them; as a proof of which the former was publicly burned in the camp; and they are said upon this occasion to have changed their colors, from a plain red ground, which they had hitherto used, to a flag with thirteen stripes, as a symbol of the number and union of the Colonies.'

Above all, we have the statement of the Italian historian, Charles Botta, in his monumental work on the American Revolution, that when the King's speech was received, together with the news that the petition of Congress had been rejected by the British Government, 'The whole army manifested the utmost indignation; the royal speech was burned in public by the infuriated soldiers. They changed at this time the red ground of their banners, and striped them with thirteen lists, as an emblem of the number and of the union of the Thirteen Colonies.'

These brief but authentic references to it describe accurately the design of the Grand Union flag, and suggest its origin. It was nothing in the world but the familiar Red Ensign or Meteor Flag of Great Britain, with six white stripes drawn across its field; the Union Jack in the canton remaining unchanged. And there is nothing more certain than that such origin of it was generally recognized and understood at that time.

When at last Washington compelled the British to evacuate Boston, and then transferred his army to New York, he carried the Grand Union flag with him and on July 9, following the first reading there of the Declaration of Independence, raised it over his fortifications and headquarters at the latter place. In testimony of this we have the word of Ambrose Searle, the confidential secretary of Admiral Lord Howe, commander of the British fleet that then came to New York, who wrote on July 25: 'They have set up their standard in the fort upon the southern end of the town. Their colors are thirteen stripes of red and white, alternately, with the English Union cantoned in the corner.' This flag was at what is still known as The Battery, in New York City.

The appearance of this flag in fact commanded more attention and evoked more comment, both in America and in England, than did that of the Stars and Stripes, a year and a half later. Its supreme significance was the union of the Thirteen Colonies. It did not directly indicate separation from Great Britain. On the contrary, it still retained the emblem of connection with that kingdom. But every thoughtful man in America, and many of those in England, realized that union of the Colonies was a step toward independence. The flag served notice upon the British Government that it must speedily and satisfactorily reverse its policy toward the Colonies and grant their demands for abatement of their grievances, or face their united revolt and the dissolution of the Empire.

So came into being our first national flag, which for the first six months of 1776 was the flag of the United Colonies, and on July 4 became the flag of the United States, or, as John Paul Jones called it, the 'Flag of America.' It was the flag under which the British were driven out of Boston, under which the Declaration of Independence was adopted, under which America was irrevocably committed to revolution and complete separation from Great Britain and the United Colonies renamed the United States, and under which was conducted that opening campaign of the war which attracted the attention of all Europe and which convinced all clear-sighted men that the illustrious Chatham was right when he said to the British Government, 'You cannot conquer America!' That flag had a lifetime of only a scant year and a half. But in that time it wrote in advance the history of the next century and a half, and opened the way *ad astra per aspera* — the way through the stripes of war to the stars of glory.

CHAPTER VI

'OUR FLAG ON THE SEAS'

MUCH controversy has long existed concerning the first use of the American flag at sea, the officers who first used it, and the ships on which it was first borne. In trying to set the record right, it will be necessary to begin with a determination of what is to be regarded as the first American flag; and that surely, as we have already seen, must be the Grand Union. We must also determine what were the first American ships; and must give that distinction to the five vessels which were commissioned by the Congress in December, 1775; of which ships John Adams, a member of the Marine Committee of the Congress, said: 'The first was named Alfred, in honor of the founder of the greatest navy that ever existed; the second, Columbus, after the discoverer of this quarter of the globe; the third, Cabot, after the discoverer of the northern part of this continent; the fourth, Andrea Doria, in honor of the great Genoese admiral; and the fifth, Providence, the name of the town where she was purchased, and the residence of Governor Hopkins and his brother Esek, whom we appointed the first captain.' The Alfred, the flagship, upon which the flag was first raised, was formerly the Black Prince, a staunch English merchant ship, whose owner and captain, John Barry, had turned it over to the Congress for naval use. Esek, or Ezekiel, Hopkins, Commodore of this fleet, was the first commander to use the Grand Union flag, and his first lieutenant, John Paul Jones, was the first actually to raise the flag with his own hands. When this fleet left the Delaware, on February 17, 1776, the order of the day prescribed that the vessels should carry, 'Saint George's ensign with stripes at the mizzen peak,' obviously the Grand Union flag in the place of honor; and also 'the standard at the maintop,' doubtless the Rattlesnake flag. A British writer at New Providence, who witnessed the operations of the fleet at that island, said in the 'London

Ladies' Magazine' that the colors of the American ships were 'striped under the Union with thirteen stripes, and their standard a rattlesnake' — exactly according with the order of the day already quoted. The first naval operation under the flag was the successful descent of this fleet upon New Providence on March 15, 1776, when two small vessels were captured without a struggle, and large stores of artillery and ammunition were taken. On March 17 the fleet set out on its return, bringing the booty, and the Governor of the island as a prisoner.

John Barry, the former merchant captain of the Black Prince, was commissioned as a captain in the American Navy in February, 1776, after Commodore Hopkins's fleet had sailed, and raised the Grand Union flag on the brig Lexington. With it he encountered, on April 17, off the Capes of Virginia, the British brig Edward. A spirited conflict ensued, in which the British vessel suffered heavy losses, was reduced to a helpless wreck, and was compelled to surrender. As Hopkins's captures, a month before, had been effected without fighting, Barry's engagement seems to have won for him the honor of having fought the first naval battle under the flag and with a commission from Congress, and of having been the first to compel a British warship to strike colors to the American flag. There were earlier operations than these, entitled to honorable remembrance, but they were under State flags and State commissions, or under those of Washington as Commander-in-Chief, and not under the flag and the commission of the Continental Congress.

John Adams, certainly a foremost authority, claimed that the flag was first raised by Captain John Manley, and that the British flag was first struck to him. Manley's flag was not, however, the Grand Union, but the Pine Tree banner of Massachusetts, and he was not commissioned by the Congress, but, as we have already seen, by Washington. Before it began commissioning vessels of its own, the Congress authorized Washington to do so at his discretion, and in consequence, during January, 1776, he sent out a fleet of six vessels, of which the Commodore was John Manley, captain of the Hancock, of whom we have already heard as the author of the Rhode Island flag. It is a matter of record, however, that these vessels were all under the Pine Tree flag and no other. Even before this time, on November 29, 1775, Captain Manley, under a Massachusetts commission, with the schooner Lee, captured the British transport Nancy, laden with artillery and ammunition, and ten days later he defeated and drove off a British schooner of eight guns and captured the two vessels which it was convoying — the ship Jenny and the brig Hannah, both laden with valuable stores.

Thus we may dispose of the question of priority in this fashion: John Manley, under a Massachusetts commission and under the Pine Tree banner, was the first to make a British naval vessel strike her flag. John Paul Jones was the first to raise the Grand Union or American flag on a ship of war. Ezekiel Hopkins was the first commander, under a commission of the Congress, to carry the Grand Union flag in naval operations and to make a capture under it. John Barry was the first, under a commission of the Congress and under the Grand Union flag, to fight a battle with a British warship and make it strike its colors. These may be regarded as fundamental data in considering the much and often acrimoniously debated question, Who was the Father of the American Navy?

The first vessel to secure for the Grand Union flag a salute from a foreign power was the Andrea Doria, under Captain Isaiah Robinson, which went to the island of Saint Eustatius, in the Dutch West Indies, to procure arms. There, on November 16, 1776, she saluted the Dutch flag, and received for the American flag a salute in return.

Finally, the first vessel to display the Grand Union flag in European waters was the ill-fated brig Reprisal, under Captain Lambert Wickes. She sailed from Philadelphia in September, 1776, for France, carrying Benjamin Franklin as the American Minister to that country. On the way she captured two British ships and took them into a French port as prizes. But as France was still a neutral nation, the prizes were ordered instantly to quit French waters, and the Reprisal was put under bonds to do the same at an early date. On her return trip to America the Reprisal foundered off the coast of New-foundland and all on board, excepting only the cook, were lost. It is with apparent authority recorded that the stripes of the Reprisal's flag were yellow and white, a circumstance which has not been explained.

The Grand Union flag was displayed in the summer of 1776 by Benedict Arnold on the Royal Savage in Lake Champlain, and in various other places, on sea and land. It was recog-nized as the authentic American flag, representing all the thirteen Colonies, or States, as they had become, and as there-fore a potentially national ensign.

CHAPTER VII

THE STARS AND STRIPES

THE Grand Union flag served the American patriots well. But because of that very fact, because of the very deeds which were performed beneath its folds, it was necessary that it be laid aside and replaced with a new standard. The Grand Union flag indeed displayed in its thirteen stripes united on a single field the symbols of the Thirteen States united in a single nation. But it also displayed in the canton the King's Colors, the Union Jack, a token of subordination to the British Crown and union with the kingdom of Great Britain. But that union had been severed, that subordination renounced forever, wherefore their token must be banished from the flag. It was in such circumstances, and for such a reason, that the Stars and Stripes came into being.

There had been antecedents, as we have seen; so that the Stars and Stripes came as one of a logical and connected series. Yet so far as the records of the Continental Congress indicate it came suddenly and unheralded. It is an interesting circumstance that the annals of Congress bear no mention of any other flag, or of action regarding any. There is no reference even to the Grand Union flag. There have long been legends, which we shall presently consider, to the effect that a committee was appointed to design a flag, that it did so and had had a specimen made, and reported and exhibited it to Congress, with an explanation of the significance of its colors and pattern. Such may have been the case. But the annals of the Continental Congress give no hint of it. On June 3, 1777, the President of the Congress reported that a friendly Indian tribe had sent to him some strings of wampum and had requested in return the gift of a flag of the United States. Presumably he gave them one of the then existing flags, the Grand Union. It does not appear that this incident had any relation to the action of the Congress eleven days later. There is no hint of it in the record. But suddenly, without any preliminary report or a word of discussion, comes the announcement of the adoption of a resolution creating the Stars and Stripes.

There is not even an intimation of the inspiration or origin of the resolution, or of the proposer of it. At the same session, however, both preceding and following closely after the Flag Resolution, though in no way connected with it, there were several others relating to naval affairs; wherefore it is at least a plausible assumption that they all alike proceeded from that Marine Committee which then served the purpose of a Navy Department. In that case it is not improbable that, as some traditions tell and as some circumstances suggest, John Adams was the author of the Flag Resolution. It sounds like him, in its directness, brevity, and emphasis.

It was Saturday, June 14, 1777. Congress was in session at Philadelphia, whither it had returned from its flight to Baltimore, after Washington's victories at Trenton and Princeton had for the time freed it from the menace of a British attack. On the walls of the hall hung the Grand Union flag, together with Pine Trees, Rattlesnakes, and other banners. The President, John Hancock, was in the chair. The conduct of the war engaged the attention of all members present. One resolution was adopted, appropriating various sums to three captains in the Army, 'for the use of their respective independent companies.' Another empowered the Marine Committee to act at its discretion for the disposal of the American ships in the Delaware River, in case of a successful incursion by the British. Then came the third:

RESOLVED: *That the Flag of the thirteen United States be thirteen stripes, alternate red and white: that the Union be thirteen stars, white in a blue field, representing a new constellation.*

That was all. That was the charter of the Stars and Stripes. There followed the reading of a letter from the Massachusetts Council of State, casting doubts upon the fitness of John Roach to continue in command of the 'Continental ship of war

Ranger'; in consequence of which two more resolutions were adopted. One of these suspended Roach from his command, pending investigation of his character and fitness. The other simply ordered: 'That Captain John Paul Jones be appointed to command the said ship Ranger.'

It does not appear that the Congress made any provision at that time for making the new flags for the Army and Navy, or even notified those services of its action. There was no 'Congressional Record' in those days, and no array of daily papers to blazon the news to the nation. The doings of Congress were told in manuscript letters from its President to Washington and other important officials; they were related by word of mouth by the members to their friends; sometimes they were published in 'broadsides,' or handbills and placards; and a few of them found leisurely publicity in the primitive weekly and other newspapers. This particular item, telling of the birth of the Stars and Stripes, does not appear to have been mentioned in the public press until about the first of August. By August 3, at any rate, it was published and was widely known. The official promulgation of the order, however, over the signature of the Secretary of the Congress, was not made until September 3, some time after the Flag had actually been used in at least one military engagement.

Perhaps the most noteworthy and the most significant circumstance connected with this great historical event was the apparent absence of comment upon it in Congress or elsewhere, either before or after its achievement. We cannot suppose that the adoption of a new national flag was not regarded as a matter of interest. The first raising of the Grand Union flag had been copiously mentioned in private correspondence and otherwise. That the discarding of it and the substitution of the Stars and Stripes elicited no comment, either approving or disapproving, must be considered extraordinary, and explicable only on the ground that there was practically unanimous agreement upon the propriety and felicity of such action. Those were highly controversial times, when men were quick to criticise and to condemn whatever was displeasing to them. The absence of criticism of the Stars and Stripes is therefore not merely pleasant to remember, but also has a direct and conclusive bearing, as we shall presently see, upon some of the legends which have arisen concerning the origin of the Flag — legends which may have been incited and encouraged by the absence of authentic records on the subject. In this case, paradoxical as it may seem, the lack of records is itself a record of a peculiarly convincing kind.

Significant, too, is the contrast between the wording of the Flag Resolution, already quoted, and that of the description of the British Union Jack, as later constituted, given by the College of Heralds, to wit:

'Azure the crosses saltire of Saint Andrew and Saint Patrick quarterly per saltire countercharged argent and gules, the latter fimbriated of the second, surmounted by the Cross of Saint George fimbriated as the saltire.'

Of a truth, America was done with heraldry as well as with royalty.

CHAPTER VIII

'A NEW CONSTELLATION'

As if to make up for the lack of discussion of the Stars and Stripes at the time of its adoption, in later years veritable floodgates of talk, speculations, invention and what not were opened; much of which output has been instinct with little wisdom.

There have, for example, been half a dozen stories, theories, or claims put forward, concerning the origin of the stripes in the field. In the Stars and Stripes these, of course, were simply copied or retained from the Grand Union flag, so we get back to the question of their origin in that banner. Despite the convincing implications in the utterances of that time, three principal theories have been advanced, attributing the design respectively to the flag of the Netherlands with its three broad red, white and blue stripes, or, as the late William Eliot Griffis stoutly maintained, to another Netherlands flag which bore seven stripes, one for each province; to the banner of the British East India Company, which had thirteen stripes of red and white, with Saint George's Cross in a white canton; and to the striped canton of the flag of the Philadelphia Light Horse Troop, already described. As to the first, if we imitated the Netherlands flag, we may ask why the whole field was not covered with stripes, without a canton. As to the second, the British East India Company's flag was scarcely known in America, save for a few visits at two or three ports; beside which, American patriots were not in 1777 or in 1775 looking for British examples to follow. And as to the third, a canton of blue and silver stripes was not much suggestive of a field of red and white ones.

The fact is that stripes had long been a familiar feature of flags. Scotland had one for her navy with eleven red and white stripes, with Saint Andrew's Cross in canton; and an English regiment, one of thirteen red and white stripes, with

Saint George's Cross, like that of the East India Company. The city of Rotterdam had one of eleven white and green stripes; Bremen one of nine, red and white; North Holland one of thirteen, yellow and red; and our own Rattlesnake flag in some of its forms had thirteen stripes, covering the whole field. Without special reference, then, to any one of these, nothing could have been more natural than for Americans to adopt a pattern of stripes, and by drawing six white stripes across the red field of the 'Meteor Flag of England' — as we have already quoted from the historian Botta — create a field symbolic of the Thirteen Colonies; the supreme fitness of which led to its retention in the Stars and Stripes.

Now, as to the stars. The words of the Act of Congress, 'forming a new constellation,' have been seized upon by some as meaning that one of the celestial constellations was copied into the canton of our Flag; never, apparently, stopping to reflect that that would not be a new constellation at all, but a very old one! It is even said that John Adams proposed that the Flag should bear the well-known constellation of Lyra, for the reason that the lyre, in the hands of Orpheus, was a token of harmony. Possibly that is true, since Adams's son, John Quincy Adams, when Secretary of State in Monroe's Cabinet, employed a representation of Lyra, on a scroll in the beak of an eagle, as a part of the official emblazonment on passports. But the facts are that so far as is known there never was a Flag made with the stars in the canton arranged Lyra-fashion; that there are a great many more than thirteen stars in that constellation; that there is no equality of brilliancy among them, to denote the equal sovereignty of the Thirteen States, but rather an exceptional inequality; and, of course, there is the explicit declaration of Congress that this was to be a *new* constellation.

Far simpler is what is probably the true explanation. It was necessary to provide some substitute for the crosses of the Union Jack. Indeed, it was to get rid of them that a new flag was to be made. But what should the substitute be? Obviously, it must meet requirements. It must be so different from the crosses as never to be mistaken for them. That barred out any other arrangement of crosses or anything like them. It must be something representative of all the States, and not specially associated with one. That barred out the Pine Tree. It must be something dignified and pleasing. That barred out the Rattlesnake. It must, finally, be something compara-tively simple and easy to make. And that barred out a number of designs which had actually been made and used.

Thus a company of soldiers at Newburyport, Massachu-setts, had carried a flag which had in the centre of the field a pine tree, surrounded by a circle of thirteen clasped hands. That was appropriate and effective for a single banner, on which the design was painted, or embroidered. But it would have been impracticable to make all the flags for the Army and Navy and for use in civil life of such a pattern. Another flag, used on some privateers, had a mail-clad hand grasping thirteen arrows. But that design also was difficult to make, in addition to being appropriate for only a battle flag. Again, the flag of the Philadelphia Light Horse Troop had, in addi-tion to the striped canton, a design resembling a rosette, con-sisting of thirteen floating scrolls united at the centre in a knot. That, like the other two, was far too elaborate and dif-ficult to make for common use on a national flag. As for any of the devices of heraldry, such as lions, dragons or what not, we have already suggested that there was no inclination among Americans at that time to cling to the customs and symbols of European nations.

In such circumstances it surely required no extraordinary inventive genius or imaginative inspiration to suggest the use of stars. These met every requirement. They were entirely different from the Union Jack or indeed any other flag. They were not identified with any one State. They were dignified and pleasing. They were simple and easy to make. They were not reminiscent of Old World heraldry. Moreover, from time immemorial stars had been regarded as celestial objects, symbolic of that which is exalted and divine. The references to the stars in the Book of Job, Pythagoras's theory of the 'music of the spheres,' and a thousand other passages in sacred and profane classics were familiar to the statesmen of that time, as expressive of the ineffable sublimity of the stellar firmament. What wonder, then, that those who designed the Flag decided to replace the crosses with stars, exquisitely appropriate for the blue ground of the canton?

There could have been no nobler symbols of the States. The lilies of France were suggestive of beauty and grace; the lion of England, of strength and mastery; the crescent of Islam, of a celestial body, though a minor one; the sun of Persia, of the great luminary and centre of our system. But greater, loftier by far than any of these, were the fixed stars. To liken the States of the Republic to a constellation of these was to place America upon a higher plane than any other power.

It is by no means fanciful or far-fetched to suppose that such thoughts as these were in the minds of those who designed the Stars and Stripes. At that time few other flags had ever displayed stars. Two and a half centuries before, Cortez carried in the conquest of Mexico a flag adorned with stars, but we can scarcely trace a relationship between it and the Stars and Stripes of 1777. Much more pertinent was the flag of Rhode Island, designed and carried by Captain John Manley, as already related. It had thirteen stars in a canton, but it is uncertain whether in that form it preceded or followed the Stars and Stripes. In either case, the use of stars as the chief symbols of a flag was, in June, 1777, a new thing. So was it a new thing for a nation to be founded upon the principles of the Declaration of Independence. It was fitting, then, that a new conception in human sovereignty should have a new conception in its ensign. It was not unwarranted but sublime audacity, that a people who had appealed to the laws of the Creator for the basic principles of their Government should turn to the celestial firmament itself for the symbolism of their Flag.

CHAPTER IX

THE WASHINGTON ARMS

ANOTHER tradition — if so it is worthy to be called — concerning the origin of the Stars and Stripes requires mention, but chiefly to rebuke, repudiate, and condemn it, as an intolerable reflection upon the Flag itself and upon the foremost man in American history. It has been said, and often repeated, that the design of the Flag was copied from the heraldic arms of the Washington family and of Washington himself. This seems to have been suggested by various British writers, soon after Washington's own time, and to have been intended by them as an invidious reflection upon him and upon America, which should have been resented here. But it was scarcely noticed in America until after the middle of the Nineteenth Century. Then it was very circumstantially stated by Martin Farquhar Tupper, the author of 'Proverbial Philosophy,' in one of the many poems which he wrote for the praiseworthy purpose of cultivating good feeling between America and Great Britain. At that time his writings were immensely popular in both countries, and his version of this story concerning the Flag was widely accepted as true in both England and America.

The passage in question occurs in his 'Centennial Drama,' and he attributes this use of the Washington arms to Benjamin Franklin, who was not in the Congress nor even in America at that time, but in France, but whom, in spite of that circumstance, he makes to say:

> . . . I proposed it to the Congress.
> It was the leader's old Crusading blazon.
> Washington's coat, his own heraldic shield.
> And on the spur, when we must choose a flag
> Symbolling independent unity,
> We, and not he — all was unknown to him —
> Took up his coat of arms and multiplied
> And magnified it in every way, to this
> Our glorious national banner.

The only basis of the story is the fact that the Washington arms, as shown on a mortuary tablet in Sulgrave Manor Church, on a monument in Little Saint Mary's Church, Oxford, on George Washington's own bookplate, and elsewhere, consist of a silver shield with two red bars across it and three red mullets, or spur-rowels, above them; and with a crest, not of an eagle, as some have said, but of a raven. Certainly the resemblance of that design to the American Flag or the American escutcheon is hopelessly remote. Grant that the two red and three silver bars suggest the thirteen red and white stripes, though even that is far-fetched, what else is to be said? The three mullets, though shaped as we now form the stars of the Flag, were not meant as stars at all; each of them was pierced with a central hole; they were red instead of white; they were on a silver instead of a blue field; and there was no touch of blue anywhere on the arms. Half a dozen other heraldic escutcheons might be named which bear a stronger resemblance to our Flag. That of the famous Douglas family, for example, shows white stars on a blue ground; and the Dufferin, Drogheda, Haddington, Kinnaird, Normanby and other arms also display mullets or stars.

While there is not a scintilla of evidence or testimony to substantiate the tradition in question, the circumstantial evidence against it is simply overwhelming. If the stripes were suggested by the five bars on the Washington shield, were those of the Grand Union flag thus suggested? And those of the Rattlesnake flag? And those of the flag of the Philadelphia Light Horse Troop? And those of the various striped flags of European countries and cities, which we have recalled? Why were not the stars placed in a row along the upper stripe, as on the Washington arms, instead of in a canton? Why were they not made red instead of white? And why was blue introduced, a color unknown to the arms? The only possible answers to these questions hopelessly discredit the tradition.

Then there is the matter of the resolution of Congress prescribing the Flag. It is not for a moment to be believed that it would have been drafted as it was, with the reference to 'a new constellation,' if the Flag was intended to be merely a development of the arms, and the stars an imitation of the mullets. The resolution in such circumstances would have been a flagrant lie, through both *suppressio veri* and *suggestio falsi*. The Continental Congress had its faults, but we are scarcely ready to believe that it unanimously and without demur connived at foisting upon the country a spurious flag, designed under false pretences.

Moreover, if Congress had done such a thing, there was somebody else to be reckoned with; namely, George Washington, who at that time was still, under an Act of Congress, invested with dictatorial authority. Everything that we know of his character, his tastes, his temperament, repudiates the suggestion that he sought or would have permitted any such personal exploitation. It is a matter of record that he once wrote, in answer to questions about his family and its arms: 'This is a subject to which I confess I have paid very little attention ... The arms enclosed in your letter are the same that are held by the family here.' It is impossible to doubt that he would have forbidden with all possible emphasis any such use of his family escutcheon. That the Congress would have adopted the design against his will, and that he would then have accepted the Flag for use in the Army under his command, is a theory simply fantastic in its folly. We cannot for a moment countenance it, unless we are to reverse our entire conception of Washington, and regard him as vain, egotistical, self-seeking and hypocritical; which, to quote the familiar phrase of Euclid, is absurd.

Finally, if the Congress had been capable of so disreputable a trick, and if Washington had been the sneak and hypocrite that the story implies, there would still have been the formidable obstacle of his enemies. For enemies he had, in Congress and out of it, especially at that time. Horatio Gates and the whole Conway Cabal, with a numerous following in Congress, were all bitterly hostile to him, and were watching night and day for opportunities of criticising him and discrediting him with the people. It is inconceivable that they would have neglected this opportunity to raise the cry that he was making his own personal arms the national ensign, and was thus preparing to make himself the sovereign of America. It is inconceivable that in after time, when faction went raving mad in the last years of Washington's Administration, Duane and the others who lampooned and vilified him in the press would have neglected to reproach him for foisting his arms into the National Flag. But nowhere is there a trace of any such criticism; nor is there in all the writings of his time a single hint that Washington had anything to do with the designing of the Flag, or that the design which was adopted had the slightest relationship to his coat of arms.

That story, entirely alien in its origin, must therefore be dismissed as without even a shadow of justification in truth, and must be regretted, as unworthy and as an aspersion upon the dignity of the Flag and upon the integrity of the Continental Congress and of Washington himself. We need not assume that it was thus intended, although some of the British writers who first put it forward did indulge in cynical and contemptuous reflections, to Washington's discredit. But we must not say that of Tupper, who was chiefly responsible for the wide circulation and acceptance of it. Despite the commonplace tone of his best-known work, and the light esteem in which literary critics have held it, he was a man of pure, generous, and chivalric soul, whose benevolent impulses and zeal for Anglo-American friendship outran his discretion. We must reject his story, and regret his folly, while we gratefully regard the man.

CHAPTER X

THE BETSEY ROSS FLAG

ANOTHER story, concerning the making of the first Flag and its presentation to the Congress — incidentally directly contradicting Tupper's Washington arms story — demands more respectful and sympathetic attention, though not entire credence. It is to the effect that in May or June, 1776, George Washington, Robert Morris and George Ross were constituted a committee to design a national flag; that they called upon Elizabeth Griscom Ross, widow of George Ross's nephew, John, and asked her — she being an expert and professional needlewoman — to make a flag from a design drawn by Washington; that she did so, first insisting upon making the stars five pointed instead of six pointed; that the stars were placed by Washington in a circle in the field in imitation of King Arthur's Round Table, to denote the equality of the States, and that Washington then personally showed that flag to the Congress, for its adoption, saying as he did so: 'We take the stars from heaven, and the red from our Mother Country, separating it by white stripes thus showing that we have separated from her; and the white stripes shall go down to posterity representing liberty.'

Now it is true that Washington was in Philadelphia from May 23 to June 5, 1776, having been summoned thither by the Congress to confer with it concerning the operations of the Army and perhaps the proposed Declaration of Independence. But it is impossible that the Flag was then presented to and adopted by the Congress, because we have the indisputable record that it was adopted by the Congress just a year later, and that meantime the Grand Union flag continued to be used. We simply cannot believe that the Stars and Stripes was designed and presented to the Congress in June, 1776, and not adopted until a full year later. Moreover, it is impossible that Washington should have said in June, 1776, that we had separated from the Mother Country, because the Declaration of Independence had not at that date been adopted. Nor is there any hint, in the Journal of the Continental Congress, that such a committee was appointed, or that the proposed flag was reported and shown to the Congress. We must therefore regard all that part of the story as seriously mistaken if not wholly apocryphal.

Nor can it be contended that it is all true save for an error in the year, which was 1777 instead of 1776. It is true that the Congress adopted the Stars and Stripes in June, 1777. But that Flag was not at that time designed and ordered made by Washington, nor shown to the Congress by him with any such speech, for the reason that he was not then in Philadelphia. It is a matter of indisputable record that from May 3 to May 28 he was at Morristown, New Jersey, and that from May 29 to June 14, the day on which the Flag Resolution was adopted by the Congress, he was at Middlebrook. Therefore he could have had nothing to do, unless possibly through correspondence, with the making, reporting, and adoption of the Flag.

The statement has been made that the Stars and Stripes actually came into existence in June, 1776, before the Declaration of Independence, and was widely used from that time forward. Then why was it necessary for the Congress a year later to pass a resolution adopting that Flag, and describing its stars as forming a 'new constellation'? And why did not Washington say something about it in the letter which he wrote to General Putnam on June 6, shortly after the date of his alleged designing of the Stars and Stripes, directing that the colonels of the Army should 'select colors for their regiments'?

As to the arrangement of the stars in a circle, it is to be observed that there is no authentic record of Washington's ever having said a word to that effect; there is no hint of it in the resolution of Congress; and there is no trace of any Flag of that pattern which was made at that time. On the contrary, the oldest specimens of the Stars and Stripes in existence, including one carried by John Paul Jones in the famous battle off Flamborough Head, all have the stars arranged in rows, as in the Flag of the present day, or in an arch.

Nevertheless, it is impossible altogether to dismiss the story of Betsey Ross as a maker of American Flags and not improbably of the first Stars and Stripes. The story of her connection with that memorable event was related, substantially as we have here recalled it, by William J. Canby, in 1870, in an address before the Pennsylvania Historical Society. He was a grandson of Mrs. Ross, and was eleven years old when she died in his parents' home, and he declared that he had himself heard the story from the lips of that venerable woman herself. Moreover, he had heard it in detail from his mother and her two sisters, daughters of Mrs. Ross.

So circumstantial a story cannot be lightly dismissed, though neither is it necessarily to be entirely believed; at any rate when some details of it are obviously in error. There is official record, of May 29, 1777, that Betsey Ross did make 'ship's colors' for the Pennsylvania Navy Board, and it is certain that she continued that occupation after the adoption of the Stars and Stripes in June, or rather after its promulgation in September, 1777; and that one of her daughters, Mrs. Clarissa Wilson, succeeded to the business and carried it on until as late as 1857. Nor will it be unfitting to continue for all time to cherish her memory, and to preserve the little cottage in which she lived and worked. There is doubtless some truth in her story, while those parts of it which are erroneous, and which may be charged to fallible memory, errors in oral repetition, or other causes, are at least innocent of harmful reflection upon either the Flag or any one concerned with it.

As for the alleged but unauthenticated words of Washington, interpreting the significance of the colors of the Flag, they are to be contrasted with the words of a report which was presented to Congress in relation to a proposed design for the Great Seal of the United States, thus: 'White signifies purity and innocence; Red, hardness and valor; Blue, vigilance, perseverance, and justice.'

Our present commendable interest in the Flag makes it by contrast seem strange that the Continental Congress paid so little attention to it. We have already noted that the resolution of June 14, 1777, gave no directions as to the arrangement of the stars, nor did it prescribe the proportions of the Flag. Epochal as the enactment now seems to us, the Congress esteemed it so lightly that it took no pains to announce it to the public, but left it to leak out incidentally weeks later; while its official promulgation was still further postponed. It entirely neglected to give any instructions or make any arrangements for the manufacture of the Flag for the public services, or to make any appropriation of money for supplying Flags to the Army and Navy. So it was left to each regiment and each vessel to make or get made its Flags as best it could. Not until after the conclusion of the treaty of peace in 1783 was the making of the National Standard regarded as a function of the Government. With so little official attention and promotion did the Stars and Stripes come into existence as the American Ensign.

CHAPTER XI

AN AMERICAN HERALD?

ANOTHER story of the designer of the Flag demands attention; much older and, it must be frankly acknowledged, more strongly supported than that concerning Betsey Ross. It relates to the claims made by Francis Hopkinson. That eminent man is chiefly remembered as one of the Signers of the Declaration of Independence, from New Jersey, and as therefore a member of the Continental Congress. He was a man of literary ability, and was the author of much Revolutionary literature, his best-known work being his humorous ballad, 'The Battle of the Kegs,' describing an incident in the Delaware River during the British occupation of Philadelphia. He is also said to have been a student of the principles and practices of heraldry, and on that account to have been employed to design various devices for official seals and for the Continental currency.

In June, 1777, at the very time of the adoption of the Flag Resolution by the Congress, he was a member and chairman of the Navy Board, a body charged with practically all executive work for the Navy, under the direction of the Marine Committee. It is therefore suggested, though without any documentary or other direct evidence of a convincing character, that he was the author of the design of the Flag as then prescribed. Practically the only testimony containing any such intimation is contained in two of his own letters, addressed to the Marine Committee or, as he styled it, the Admiralty Board. The first of these, written in 1779, two years or more after the adoption of the Stars and Stripes, expressed great pleasure at the approbation which he understood the Board had given to the device which he had prepared for its official seal; and continued:

I have with great readiness upon several occasions exerted my

small abilities in this way for the public service, as I flatter myself,
to the satisfaction of those I wish to please, viz.:

The Flag of the United States of America.

Four devices for the Continental currency.

A seal for the Board of Treasury . . .

A Great Seal for the United States of America, with a Reverse.

For these services I have as yet made no charge nor received
any recompense. I now submit to your Honours' consideration
whether a quarter cask of public wine will not be a proper and
reasonable reward for these labours of fancy and a suitable encour-
agement to others of the like nature. . . .

Apparently the Board or Committee did not agree with
him that a quarter cask of wine would be 'a proper and
reasonable reward.' Whether it was influenced simply by pe-
nuriousness, or impecuniosity, or by some other motive, does
not appear. An imaginative mind might attribute to the
Board the prescience of a seer, and a consequent unwilling-
ness to pay for the Flag with something which in future years
would be prohibited and outlawed under that very Flag. At
any rate, such payment was not made, nor was a recompense
of any kind made for Hopkinson's heraldic labors. A little
later he sent another more formal bill to the Congress, demanding payment for the designs already mentioned and also
for numerous others, the first item on the list being 'The
Great Naval Flag of the United States.' The amount of the
bill was expressed not in wine but in hard cash, in the sum of
$2,700.

This was presented to the Treasury Committee, which referred it to a Board of Accounts, and the latter disapproved its
payment. Hopkinson, it said, 'was not the only person con-
sulted on those exhibitions of Fancy' and therefore was not
entitled to claim full credit for them nor to receive the full
sum charged. In addition, it expressed the somewhat em-
phatic opinion that the public was entitled to such little
assistance, given by gentlemen who already enjoyed very
considerable salaries under the Congress, without any further
payment for them. So the bill was never paid, not even in

the Continental currency the designing of which formed one
of its prominent items.

It is a matter of record that the Congress did authorize the
designing and making of a Great Seal of the United States,
and also seals for the Treasury and the Navy; but there is
nothing in the annals of that body to indicate that the work
was entrusted to Hopkinson. From July, 1776, to June, 1782,
a succession of Congressional committees, including in membership John Adams, Franklin, Jefferson, Henry Middleton,
Edward Rutledge, Elias Boudinot, and others, labored over
the task. They at times had the aid of the Secretary of the
Congress, Charles Thompson, of William Barton, of Philadelphia, and of a French artist, Du Simitière; and they produced a series of designs, chiefly fantastic and impractical —
one, the work of Jefferson, portraying the Israelites crossing
the Red Sea and the army of Pharaoh being destroyed! All
these were happily rejected by the Congress until the last.
This was chiefly designed by William Barton, under the
supervision and pretty strenuous direction of Elias Boudinot,
and was substantially the seal as it is today. It was adopted
on June 20, 1782. What part if any Hopkinson had in any
of this work does not authentically appear. But the presumption must be that it was little if any at all if, as stated, he was
skilled in heraldry, for anything more unheraldic than those
designs it would be difficult to imagine.

Benson J. Lossing, the historian of the Revolution, on the
authority of an English antiquary, stated that the design of the
Great Seal was suggested to John Adams by Sir John Prest-
wick, an English baronet who was most friendly to America;
but of this there seems to be no convincing evidence. As for
the motto on the seal, 'E Pluribus Unum,' its origin is a matter of uncertainty. It was used as a motto on the first volume
of the old 'Gentleman's Magazine' of London, which was
published before the Revolution and was familiar to Americans, and was continued in such use in successive volumes for
a hundred years thereafter. It has also been pointed out that
the words *e pluribus unus* occur in an old Latin poem, the

authorship of which is not surely known but has been ascribed to Virgil.

The original Naval seal, adopted in 1779 but discarded for another a hundred years later, was reported to the Congress by a committee consisting of John Witherspoon, Gouverneur Morris and Richard Henry Lee, and at the same time seals were adopted for the Treasury and for the War Department, which were retained for nearly a hundred years. To what extent Hopkinson was concerned with any of these is not apparent, save in his letters.

It is of interest, however, to observe that in his various writings, referring to the Flag, he calls it by no fewer than four different names, to wit: 'The Flag of the United States,' 'The Great Naval Flag of the United States,' 'The Naval Flag of the United States' and 'The Naval Flag of the States.' It is partly upon the basis of this that many have assumed that the Stars and Stripes was designed and adopted solely for the Navy and not at all for the Army. Indeed, this has been confidently stated as a fact by various writers, though on what authority does not appear. There is no recorded official reservation of the use of the Flag. And there is, of course, to the contrary effect always the plain and indisputable wording of the Flag Resolution itself, prescribing 'the Flag of the Thirteen United States.' If those words mean anything at all, they must mean that this was to be the national ensign, for universal use, on land and sea alike. And it must not be overlooked that Hopkinson himself, while calling it the 'naval flag,' also calls it, and calls it in the first instance, 'the Flag of the United States of America.'

We may regard it as sufficiently well established that Hopkinson was concerned in the making of the Stars and Stripes, probably in an intimate and important manner; though precisely to what extent or in what way it is impossible to determine. That he was its sole maker seems to be denied by the statement of the Board of Accounts, already quoted. That he conceived the entire design is obviously impossible of maintenance, since the design in most respects had already been conceived and had been in actual existence for nearly a year and a half. The colors, red, white, and blue, had already been established. So had the red and white stripes. So had the blue canton. At most, then, the conception and the act of creating the new Flag amounted to nothing more than the substitution of thirteen white stars for the Cross of Saint George and the Saltire of Saint Andrew. That was, however, a most felicitous thing, and it is the measure of the utmost credit for design that can be awarded to Hopkinson or, for that matter, to anybody in the case.

There remains the minor suggestion that Hopkinson's part in the flag-making was that of a skilled draughtsman and colorist, and that he merely made a drawing of the design upon which the Naval Board or the Marine Committee or some other unnamed authority had agreed; or possibly that he procured the fabrication of an actual flag, in silk or bunting. Some plausibility is given to this by the fact, commonly stated and not disputed, that he was a student of heraldry and may therefore be assumed to have been skilled in such work. But he did not carry his knowledge of heraldry, or exercise his authority, so far as to insist upon conforming the Flag to all the principles and laws of that ancient art. We may, however, enjoy this consolation, copious and convincing, that in violating some of those laws the American ensign enjoys the goodly companionship of the great majority of the national standards of the world; and that, moreover, it was most fitting for it to violate them, since it was itself the most outstanding token and symbol of a new era, in which heraldry and that for which it stood were obsolete.

CHAPTER XII

FIRST APPEARANCES

THE stories concerning the designing of the Flag are numerous; but they are far surpassed in both number and variety by those concerning its first public display and its first use in battle. And of these latter it is not as easy to dispose, whether affirmatively or negatively, as of the former. It will be profitable, however, to consider the more important ones *seriatim*, in chronological order, and see upon what — if any — basis of known fact they rest, and with what circumstantial or inferential evidence they are supported, or on the other hand what evidence there is against them; and to do this even at the risk or cost of discrediting some fondly cherished traditions.

It has been stated with much apparent assurance that immediately upon its adoption by the Congress, on June 14, 1777, the Flag was raised above Washington's headquarters at Camp Middlebrook, in New Jersey. Doubtless this seems, on the face of it, the natural and appropriate thing to have done; and it would be impossible to prove positively that it was not done. There is not a word or a hint in the available record concerning it, in either affirmation or denial. There is no mention of it. But that lack of mention, in either official records or private correspondence and journals — which latter were copious — is significant. There was abundant mention of the first raising of the Grand Union flag at Charlestown and Cambridge; and it seems extraordinary that there was none of the raising of the Stars and Stripes at Middlebrook, if it was then and there raised. We must remember that, while adopted on June 14, the Flag was not officially promulgated by the Congress until September 3. That is indisputable. There is no good reason, therefore, to suppose that Washington was officially informed of the adoption of the Flag before the latter date. His correspondence contains no hint of it. There is no indication that he knew anything about it until about the first of August, when the first unofficial news of the event was published in the newspapers. Moreover, even if he had learned unofficially of the action of the Congress, he was entirely too punctilious in matters of etiquette to make and display the new Flag until official promulgation of it had been made and notified to him. Regrettable as it may be, and even though it may be resented by those who have cherished the Middlebrook tradition, it is necessary at least to doubt very gravely whether the Stars and Stripes ever flew above that famous and important encampment.

Because of the brilliant and decisive repulse by Washington's troops of the British advance toward Middlebrook, with designs upon Philadelphia, in June, 1777, and the consequent retirement of the British from New Jersey in the last days of that month, the first anniversary of the Declaration of Independence, on July 4, was joyously and elaborately celebrated by the Congress and the people of Philadelphia. Concerning this, Bancroft in his 'History of the United States' says explicitly:

The bells rung all day and all the evening; ships, row-galleys, and boats showed the new Flag of the thirteen United States: thirteen stripes, alternate red and white; for the union thirteen stars, white in a blue field, representing a new constellation.

Here again appears the notion that the Stars and Stripes was distinctively a naval flag, since Bancroft mentions its display upon vessels but not upon buildings, not even above the meeting-place of the Congress. However, he makes no mention, either, of any authority for the statement that it was thus displayed, and his report does not seem to be corroborated by any contemporary narrative of that time. It is necessary, therefore, to remit his account to the category of those stories which, like that of Middlebrook, are so appropriate that they really ought to be true, but which have in fact no credible foundation but, on the contrary, are discredited by circumstantial evidence.

The claim has been made, with patriotic zeal, that a hastily improvised flag was made and carried by the American troops in the battle at Hubbardton, Vermont, on July 7, 1777. This has been most carefully examined by John Spargo, the Vermont historian, with the result that he dismisses it as entirely unworthy of credence. The fact that the story refers to the flag as having been made, in part, from an officer's blue cloak, seems to connect it with the later and at least partially authentic account of the making and use of a flag at Fort Schuyler, which we shall presently consider. It remains to be repeated that, according to the carefully kept Journal of Dr. James Thacher, of Albany, New York, the authenticity of which has not been impeached, the first knowledge of the Stars and Stripes did not reach that city until about August 3. On that date he wrote: 'It appears by the papers that Congress resolved on the 14th of June last that the Flag of the United States be thirteen stripes, alternate red and white; that the Union be thirteen stars, white on a blue field.' Now if that was not known at Albany until August 3, it is incredible that it was known nearly a month earlier at Hubbardton, a place much more remote from Philadelphia and much less in touch with the progress of affairs. The same inexorable logic of time and place compels us to dismiss also the story of the Flag's having been displayed at Fort Anne, on July 9, 1777; a story which seems to rest upon a 'diary' which was written some years afterward by a man who was not present at the events he describes. In fact, any account or tradition of the use of the Flag before about the first of August, 1777, at which date news of its adoption was first made public, must be regarded with incredulity, unless and until it is supported with such proof as has not yet been adduced.

Next comes the far more important and circumstantial story of the making and use of the Stars and Stripes at Fort Schuyler, formerly known as Fort Stanwix, near the site of the present city of Rome, New York, on August 3, 1777; a story which has received much official credence. Of it, indeed, practically everything must be accounted as historically true, with the exception of a single detail, which happens, for the present purpose, to be the most important of all. As a part of Burgoyne's campaign a British and Indian force under General St. Leger was sent to seize Fort Schuyler, which was held by a small force under Colonel Peter Gansevoort and Lieutenant-Colonel Marinus Willett. On the evening of August 2 a company of Massachusetts troops arrived as reënforcements, bringing — so the story runs — news of the adoption of the Stars and Stripes. Instantly it was resolved that the garrison must have such a flag to fight under the next day, when an attack by the enemy in force was expected. So during that night a flag was improvised, of which Lieutenant-Colonel Willett has left an indisputable account. 'The white stripes,' he wrote, as commonly quoted, 'were cut out of ammunition shirts furnished by the soldiers; the blue out of the camlet cloak taken from the enemy at Peekskill; while the red stripes were made of different pieces of stuff procured from one and another of the garrison.' There is a tradition that the red came from the red flannel petticoats of some of the officers' wives. The blue cloak belonged to Captain Abraham Swartwout, and there is in existence his letter asking to be paid for it or to be provided with another cloak.

The next day the fighting began. Lieutenant-Colonel Willett led a gallant sortie against the enemy on August 6, to divert their attention from General Herkimer, who was on his way thither; routed them, and captured five of their flags. Then, says Botta, in his History, 'he led back his whole corps without loss, and raised a trophy composed of the conquered arms and baggage, under the American standard, which waved upon the walls of the fortress.'

There is no reason to doubt, then, that a flag was thus hastily made on the night of August 2–3, and that it was thereafter displayed on the walls of Fort Schuyler; though it was not carried by the troops in their successful sortie. The one important point which is in doubt is whether it was the Stars

and Stripes, or the old Grand Union flag. Since the Stars and
Stripes had been adopted by the Congress nearly two months
before, it has been hastily concluded that it was of course the
flag which the garrison of Fort Schuyler made. Examination
of the record fails, however, to disclose the slightest proof of
that assumption, while the circumstantial evidence seems to
be quite to the contrary.

There is no authority whatever for saying that the Massachusetts troops brought news of the Stars and Stripes. That
is sheer assumption. In Botta's History there is no suggestion
that it was the Stars and Stripes, but merely the 'American
standard.' Remembering how carefully he described the
Grand Union flag in his account of its raising at Prospect Hill,
it seems very strange that he said nothing about the design
of the Fort Schuyler flag if it was indeed the new one. Still
more significant is it that Marinus Willett in his very circumstantial written account of the incident makes no mention of
its being the newly adopted Stars and Stripes, which we must
think he surely would have done, had it been that flag. Indeed, if we examine the precise text of his narrative, instead
of merely the brief and incomplete quotation which is familiar
to the public, we find strong reasons for believing that it was
not the Stars and Stripes, but the Grand Union flag.

In the first place he says: 'The Fort had never been Sup-
plyed with a Flagg.' That is, it had never had a Grand Union
or any other flag, save perhaps the State flag or regimental
emblems. Next: 'The importance of having one on the arrival
of the Enemy had set our ingenuity to work.' Not, be it noted,
any news of Stars and Stripes brought by the Massachusetts
troops, nor any desire to have the new flag, but merely the
thought that when the enemy attacked it the fort must display
the national ensign, whatever that might be. He writes not a
word about the making or use of any stars, though as they
would have been the novel feature of the flag and the hardest
to make, we should think he surely would have had something
to say about them. Instead, he speaks of 'the white stripes'
and 'the red stripes,' and of 'the blue strips.' There is no

mention of a star, and there is no mention of the blue ground of the canton. The phrase 'blue strips' is significant. There are no such things in the Stars and Stripes; but there were in the Grand Union flag. Certainly, had the garrison been making a Stars and Stripes they would have cut a whole big square out of Swartwout's 'camlet cloak' for the blue canton, on which to sew white stars. They would not have cut it into 'strips.' Yet Willett says explicitly that 'the blue strips [were cut] out of the cloak.' Finally, he speaks of it not as the new 'Flag of the Thirteen United States,' but as 'the Continental Flag.'

To this we may add two further bits of cumulative testimony. Lieutenant William Colbrath, who was present on the occasion, agrees with Willett and leaves it on written record that it was 'a Continental Flag' that was raised. That is certainly suggestive of the Grand Union flag, which had for a year and a half been thus known. It conveys no suggestion of a flag of a new design, which was officially called 'the Flag of the United States.' Also, and finally, there is the testimony of John McGraw, a soldier of the New York State troops, who was at Fort Schuyler in the fall of that year. He decorated his powder horn with artistic skill, with the inscription: 'Fort Schuyler, December 25, 1777, J. McGraw,' and with a plan of the fort, upon one bastion of which a flag was flying. And the flag which he there engraved with painstaking care and accuracy was not a Stars and Stripes but a Grand Union flag, though with only the Saltire of Saint Andrew in the canton.

It is always an ungrateful and often an odious task to deny a popular belief and to destroy a beautiful tradition of patriotism; and it is something that must always be undertaken with the utmost circumspection, and even then with reluctance and regret. But while absolute proof is lacking and probably must always be lacking, the great preponderance of indications certainly seems to be to the effect that the flag so gallantly made and upheld at Fort Schuyler was not the Stars and Stripes.

It will be pertinent and fitting to add a word concerning the

name of the fort in question, which we have called Schuyler
instead of Stanwix, though the latter is, unfortunately and
inexcusably, the common appellation. Originally, during the
Indian wars, it was called Stanwix, after a British officer.
But when the Revolution began and it became an American
stronghold against the British, it was in 1776 rebuilt and renamed Fort Schuyler, after the gallant General of that name
who was in command in that region. As early, at least, as
February 2, 1777, it was called Schuyler in official docu-
ments, and it still bore that name six months later, when
St. Leger vainly attacked it and the flag episode occurred.
Indeed, it always thereafter was officially known as Fort
Schuyler. It is true that it was also sometimes called Stanwix.
But that was done in part by those who had not yet learned
of the change of name to Schuyler, and in part — probably
in chief part — by the underlings and sycophants of Horatio
Gates, as a feature of his sordid and malignant intrigue
against the man whose character and ability he meanly
envied. To call it Stanwix now is — though of course un-
wittingly — to countenance and continue Gates's aspersions
upon one of the noblest figures in New York's Revolutionary
history. Fort Schuyler it was when Gansevoort and Willett
defended it against St. Leger, and Fort Schuyler it should
ever be in grateful memory.

John Paul Jones's Flag

Bennington Flag

Guilford Flag

Maryland Militia Flag

Fifteen Stripe Flag

Big Star Flag

CHAPTER XIII

BENNINGTON AND OTHERS

A FORTNIGHT after Fort Schuyler came Bennington. At the former a diversion was sought for Burgoyne's relief at the westward, and at the latter the operation was repeated at the eastward, to meet with still more disastrous failure. The battle was fought on August 16, 1777, and in connection with it there were used two flags which are still in existence. One was a green flag, with a blue canton containing thirteen white stars painted on it, of different sizes and irregularly placed. Of it the canton is still in existence, with a narrow fringe of green field clinging to it. Very positive and coherent traditions of the family of General Stark are to the effect that this was his battle flag at Bennington. Obviously, however, it was not the Stars and Stripes. The green field, instead of red and white stripes, was like that of a flag formerly used by the militia of Newbury, Massachusetts, and was also suggestive of the 'Green Mountain Boys,' who at that time were known by that name.

The other Bennington flag is still in existence, almost uninjured, in the possession of the Bennington Battle Monument and Historical Association, and is indubitably a Stars and Stripes, though of a form and pattern strange to our eyes. It is ten feet in length and only five and a half in width, quite different from the standard proportions of the flag. There are seven white stripes instead of six, and six red stripes instead of seven, so that the top and bottom stripes are white instead of red. That arrangement was also adopted by the French artist and engravers who made the original certificate of membership of the Society of the Cincinnati in Paris in 1783, and is to be seen in other French representations of the flag. The explanation is that it is in accordance with the technical rules of heraldry, while our present placing of the stripes is not.

But the canton of this Bennington flag is of greatest interest.

It is larger than that of our present flag, spanning nine stripes instead of seven. It is of blue, and contains thirteen white stars. But instead of being five-pointed with one point directed upward the stars are seven-pointed with one point directed downward. Eleven of them are arranged in an arch, springing from the two lower corners of the canton and rising about two-thirds of its height, and the other two, much larger, are in the upper corners. Underneath the arch are the large Arabic numerals 76, which we may assume to be a contraction of the date of Independence, 1776. This remarkable flag was, according to credible tradition, in the charge of Lieutenant Nathaniel Fillmore, a soldier in the Battle of Bennington and the grandfather of Millard Fillmore, President of the United States. During the War of 1812 he gave it to his nephew, Septa Fillmore, who in turn gave it to his nephew, Philetus P. Fillmore, and he passed it on to his nephew, Franklin Bosworth Fillmore. The last-named left it to his daughter, Mrs. W. H. Wilson, and she presented it to the Bennington Battle Monument and Historical Association in whose museum it now reposes.

It has seemed worth while to rehearse these details, which were secured with much pains by John Spargo, because of the coherent and consistent oral tradition of the use of the flag at Bennington which was transmitted through successive generations from Nathaniel Fillmore to Maude Fillmore Wilson. No other tradition of an early flag is so complete as this, or so free from suggestions of doubt and uncertainty. It must be accepted as convincing evidence that this is a flag of Revolutionary date, and the oldest now existing that bears the emblems of stars and stripes. It is difficult to explain its origin otherwise than in an attempt to fulfil the resolution of the Congress of June 14. That resolution prescribed the order of the stripes as 'alternate red and white,' but to make them white and red instead probably seemed a permissible divergence. It said nothing about the arrangement of the stars, save that they would form 'a new constellation,' a prescription which the arch fulfilled certainly as well as either a circle or a series of parallel rows. Neither did it say how many points the stars were to have.

With such flags displayed at the left and right of the American line, what of the centre? It has been again and again asserted with perfect confidence that the Stars and Stripes flew above Gates's army at Saratoga, at the surrender of Burgoyne. There is, however, no record to that effect. In the accounts and other papers of the Army there are several references to the supplying of 'Continental flags,' which we must understand to mean the Grand Union, but there is no mention of the Stars and Stripes, nor does any occur in any of the diaries or letters which were written at that time. Trumbull's painting of the scene does indeed show a Stars and Stripes; but historical paintings are notoriously untrustworthy — note the 'Old Master' portraying the Crucifixion of Jesus, in which a Roman soldier standing guard at the foot of the Cross is armed with a blunderbuss!

There are, however, some strong reasons for believing that the new Flag was displayed at Saratoga. One is the personality of Horatio Gates. He was the particular pet of the ruling faction in the Congress, and was therefore more likely than Washington or any one else to be in touch with that body, to know what it had done, and to adopt the Flag which it had prescribed even in advance of its official promulgation. No sense of etiquette would have restrained him from such a course, but on the contrary his insatiable vanity would have urged him to it. Doubtless, too, his copartners in the Conway Cabal would be eager to have him thus distinguished above the commander whom he was hoping and plotting to replace. So we may credit the tradition that the wives of the officers of his army made a Stars and Stripes and presented it to Gates, to be raised over his headquarters. Another reason is stronger and more worthy. John Stark proceeded from Bennington to Saratoga, to assist Gates, and was a member of the council which accepted the surrender of Burgoyne. With him went Colonel Seth Warner and Captain Elijah Dewey and their men, who had fought under him at Bennington; and Dewey's company had in its possession the Stars and Stripes. It is scarcely conceivable that the Flag which they had fought under at Bennington was left behind. Rather may we confidently assume that it was carried by them to Saratoga.

Of the precise design of the flag which the women are said to have made for Gates, we have no inkling. It may have resembled the Bennington flag, or have had some other arrangement of the stars and stripes. In the absence of any official rules on the subject, the Flag, at least on land, for a number of years was seen in many forms. That at Bennington was one. Another was that of the North Carolina troops at Guilford Courthouse, on March 15, 1781. This measured nearly three times as long as it was wide; its canton spanned eight stripes and was of similar proportions; the stripes were red and blue; the canton was white with blue stars, and the stars were eight-pointed. Still another was that of Maryland troops at the Cowpens, the length of which was two and a half times its width, and which had twelve five-pointed stars in a circle and the thirteenth at the centre of it. Arthur Lee, one of our Commissioners to France, in September, 1778, wrote to the President of the Congress, Henry Laurens, that the colors, evidently meaning the stripes, should be white, red, and blue alternately, with a blue canton and white stars. In the spring of 1780 officers on the British fleet at Charleston, South Carolina, wrote of seeing the Stars and Stripes raised above one of the American forts, where thitherto there had been only a blue flag with thirteen stars; and a little later they wrote exultantly of seeing the Stars and Stripes pulled down and replaced with the British colors. And as late as April 24, 1783, Ezra Stiles, President of Yale College, wrote in his diary of the flag which the women of New Haven had made in honor of the peace with Great Britain. This was the Stars and Stripes but with what he erroneously described as the Arms of the United States among the stars in the canton. In fact, it was the Arms of the State of Pennsylvania, with the motto, 'Virtue, Liberty, Independence.'

There is preserved in the State House at Boston a flag

which is said to have flown over Fort Independence, in Boston Harbor, in the Revolution, as early as 1781. It is a Stars and Stripes, pure and simple, with the symbols arranged precisely as they are at the present time, or as they would be, were a Flag now made with only thirteen stars. Its fame seems to rest upon mere oral tradition rather than upon any written record; yet it is, more than most such stories, worthy of consideration. We know, as we shall presently see, that the Flag was at an early date made in precisely that form for use on the vessels of the Navy, and the intimate relations of Boston to maritime affairs strongly suggests that one of the naval ensigns may have been placed upon Fort Independence.

Two of the most positive statements concerning the early use of the Flag are that it was displayed at the skirmish at Cooch's Bridge, in Delaware, on September 3, 1777, and that it was carried by Washington's troops in the Battle of the Brandywine on September 11, eight days later. A monument relating in graven stone the former incident has been erected at Cooch's Bridge, and Rear-Admiral Preble, in his compendious history of the Flag, declares that the Stars and Stripes was 'undoubtedly' unfurled at the Brandywine. Yet for neither of these statements is there a word of documentary basis, or anything more than oral tradition. On the other hand, there is no evidence whatever to the contrary; there are no known circumstances which cast denial or even doubt upon them; wherefore we may regard it as probable that the Flag was used on those occasions — though in view of what we know about Bennington we may take exception to the claim that at Cooch's Bridge was the 'first' unfurling of the Stars and Stripes in battle. The engagement at Cooch's Bridge, it will be observed, occurred on the very day, September 3, on which the new Flag was formally promulgated by the Congress, and it may well be that the Delaware troops were prompt in obtaining a sample of the standard. On the same line of reasoning it may be supposed that a Stars and Stripes was provided for Washington himself, or was obtained by him, and was carried at the Brandywine. That there was any general adoption of the Flag by the Army is not, however, to be believed; especially since Washington wrote as late as May, 1779, nearly two years after the adoption of the Flag Resolution by the Congress, and more than a year and a half after the Brandywine, that 'it is not yet settled what is the Standard of the United States.' And it is a matter of record that the use of the Stars and Stripes as the ensign of the American Army was not prescribed nor even authorized by the Government until well on in the Nineteenth Century. It was used above forts, and it was carried by troops in a number of cases, though without official orders to that effect. But not until 1834 does it seem to have been prescribed or authorized for use in the field, and then only by the artillery — an obvious extension of the use on fortifications. In 1841 it came into use by the infantry of the Army, and finally in 1887 it was prescribed for the cavalry also. During the Civil War, from 1861 to 1865, each cavalry company was authorized to carry a small guidon consisting of the Stars and Stripes, but that order was revoked at the end of the war. The 'National Colors' used before the introduction of the Stars and Stripes into the Army was a blue field, without a canton, with the coat of arms or escutcheon of the United States in the centre; somewhat resembling the President's Flag of to-day, but without the four stars in the corners.

Perhaps a word may be profitable concerning the anachronisms which were perpetrated by artistic license in some of our historical paintings. Leutze's familiar portrayal of 'Washington Crossing the Delaware' shows Colonel Munroe, at Washington's side, holding the Stars and Stripes. Charles Wilson Peale's painting of Washington at the Battle of Trenton also shows the Stars and Stripes, with the stars arranged in a circle; and John Trumbull's picture of the Battle of Princeton represents the Stars and Stripes with twelve stars in a square around the edge of the canton and the thirteenth in the centre. Those operations all occurred nearly six months before the adoption of the Stars and Stripes, and at a time when Washington's army was undoubtedly under the Grand Union flag. But it is not improbable that the artists committed these anachronisms deliberately, with the purpose of conveying, paradoxically, through technical falsification a truer impression than would have been produced by the literal truth. For they rightly assumed that their pictures would be seen in the far future, by millions who would have forgotten or perhaps never have heard of the Grand Union flag and would therefore not understand its significance. The essential thing was, and for all time would be, to indicate that the American Flag was being carried by the American troops, and that would most surely be accomplished by portraying a flag that would be instantly recognized as the American standard by all who at any time should see it, rather than by using one which would be strange and unrecognizable, though it might be technically correct.

CHAPTER XIV

THE FLAG ABROAD

MUCH more certain than the facts concerning the first use of the Stars and Stripes on land and in battle by the American Army are those of its first appearance on the high seas and in foreign lands or waters as the ensign of the American Navy. This achievement was effected by John Paul Jones, who as flag lieutenant had first raised the Grand Union flag on Commodore Hopkins's flagship. In the very same hour that the Flag Resolution was adopted by the Congress — though not, as has been erroneously stated, in the same resolution — he was appointed to the command of the sloop of war Ranger, at Portsmouth, New Hampshire. That circumstance made a deep impression upon his partly romantic and partly fatalistic mind. 'That Flag and I,' he wrote, 'are twins; born the same day and the same hour. We cannot be parted in life or in death. So long as we can float, we shall float together. If we must sink, we shall go down as one.'

He promptly took command of the Ranger, and was for some time busy in preparing her for a transatlantic cruise. There is no record of the date on which he raised the Stars and Stripes upon her, but there is a tradition that he did so on the Fourth of July. For that tradition there is no basis in known facts, while circumstantial evidence strongly discredits it. In fact, Jones himself records that he did not go to Portsmouth until July 12. There is no reason to suppose that he knew of the adoption of the Flag until a much later date. But when he did learn of it, his fervid and impetuous disposition doubtless moved him to raise the Flag as soon as one could be provided. And apparently the provision was promptly made by the people of Portsmouth. There is a tradition which, if not verified by indisputable records, is at least plausible and is not discredited by any known facts or circumstances, that five young women of that town, with their own hands, made a

Stars and Stripes, 'from their best silk dresses.' Their names
deserve to be remembered. They were Helen Seavey, Mary
Langdon, Augusta Pierce, Caroline Chandler, and Dorothy
Hall — family names, some of them, honorably eminent in
New Hampshire history in after years. Presumably a flag
thus made from material so beautiful yet so fragile and ill-
suited to battle with Atlantic storms was reserved for the Captain's cabin, while one of more robust texture took its place at
the peak.

The Ranger, however, did not put out of port until the first
of November, 1777, and thus it was on that date that the Flag
first went upon the high seas. Thirty days later Jones reached
with her the French port of Nantes, having captured two
British ships on the way. Thus he had made four records. He
had first raised the Stars and Stripes on a naval vessel; he had
first borne it on the high seas; he had first under it captured
British vessels as prizes; and he had for the first time carried
that Flag into the waters and port of a foreign Power.

There remained, a little later, a fifth achievement, that of
securing from a foreign Power a salute to that Flag. This
was not done at Nantes. But from that port he escorted some
American vessels to Quiberon Bay, where he placed them
under the protection of the French fleet commanded by Admiral La Motte Piquet. He arrived at the entrance to that bay
on the evening of February 13, and the next morning sent in a
boat to inquire if the French Admiral would salute the American Flag. The reply was that he would do so, but that he
could not give gun for gun, but would have to salute with four
fewer guns than those with which Jones would salute the
French flag. This was a disappointment to Jones, who had
counted on getting as full a salute for the American Flag as
that which the French flag received, and he was inclined to
sail away without any saluting on either side. On inquiry,
however, he found that such was the practice and indeed the
law of France in saluting the flag of the Netherlands or any
other republic. For a republic was considered inferior in rank
to a kingdom, and to be entitled to four fewer guns in a salute.

This hesitation and the time required for inquiries and investigation as to the practice consumed the day, and it was a little after sunset on February 14, 1778, when Jones, on the Ranger, saluted the French flag with thirteen guns — one for each of the United States — and received for the American flag a salute of nine guns in reply. The next morning Jones went aboard another of the American vessels, the brig Independence, and with it sailed through the French fleet, saluting with thirteen guns, and receiving a salute of nine in return. Of this he wrote to the Marine Committee of the Congress: 'I am happy to have it in my power to congratulate on my having seen the American Flag, for the first time, recognized in the fullest and completest manner by the flag of France.'

Both these salutes were also recorded, to precisely the same effect, by Dr. Ezra Green, surgeon of the Ranger, in his diary; he also declaring that this was 'the first salute ever pay'd the American Flag.' Of course he and Jones both meant by 'the American Flag' the Stars and Stripes; since the Grand Union flag had formerly been saluted, as we have seen, by the Dutch at the island of Saint Eustatius.

There remained a sixth achievement by Jones. This was the first fight under the Stars and Stripes with a ship of the British Navy, and this occurred on April 24, 1778, when Jones with the Ranger engaged the British ship Drake, off Whitehaven, and compelled her to strike her colors. On that occasion, wrote Jones to the American Commissioner in Paris, 'the American stars were displayed on board the Ranger.'

Another achievement, by another commander, was the first invasion of a foreign land and capture of a foreign fortress, which was effected on January 28, 1778. Late the preceding evening Captain John Rathbone, commanding the sloop of war Providence, landed twenty-five men on the island of New Providence, where they were joined by nearly as many more Americans who had escaped from British prisons and were seeking an opportunity to get home. The united force made a midnight attack upon Fort Nassau and captured it, with a number of cannon and much ammunition and three hundred muskets, and raised above it the Stars and Stripes. The next morning a ship of war and five merchantmen, which had been taken as prizes by the British and which lay in the harbor, were captured. Although menaced by vastly superior forces, the Americans held the fort for two days. Then they spiked all the cannon, took the small arms and ammunition aboard the ships, and sailed away in triumph. Two of the ships were valueless, and were burned, but all the others reached the United States in safety. Thus this first warlike exploit on foreign soil crowned the Stars and Stripes with the laurels of victory.

CHAPTER XV

IN WAR AND PEACE

THE Stars and Stripes came into general use but slowly. The Congress, as we have seen, made no appropriation for the manufacture of flags, not even for the Services. It is probable, however, that the Marine Committee, or Navy Board, did order some made for the Navy, as it had done before. There is a record of payment of a small sum to Betsey Ross on May 20, 1777, for making colors for the vessels; but as that was some weeks before the adoption of the Stars and Stripes, we must assume that they were Grand Union flags that she had been making. It is certain, however, that the new Flag was borne during the remainder of the war, though not on the land as generally as on the sea.

One of its most memorable uses was made by John Paul Jones, in the famous naval battle off Flamborough Head, on September 23, 1779. It was specifically agreed between him and the French commanders of the two French ships which accompanied him and his Bon Homme Richard that all should fly the American Flag. Some writers have strangely assumed this to have been still the Grand Union flag, unmindful of three circumstances which convincingly prove it to have been the Stars and Stripes. One is, of course, the known fact that Jones carried the Stars and Stripes on the Ranger in 1777 and 1778, and it is impossible to believe that he then discarded it and resumed the Grand Union flag. Another is, that the poet, Philip Freneau, in some verses which he conceived at the time in honor of Jones and his great exploit, wrote:

> Go on, great man, to scourge the foe,
> And bid the haughty Britons know
> They to our thirteen stars shall bend.

The third circumstance is found in the very flag, or one of the flags, which Jones carried in that battle, which is fully authenticated and is still in existence. This is the Stars and Stripes, with twelve stars in the canton, arranged in four horizontal rows of three stars each. There has been much speculation over the reason for there being only twelve stars, but the mystery is probably easily solved. It is known that during the Civil War a strip of the flag, some inches wide, running across the whole end next the staff, was cut off and given to President Lincoln. This of course included a part of the canton and the ends of the six stripes below it. It is reasonable to assume that it also included the thirteenth star, for indeed that was necessary to the completeness and significance of the gift to Lincoln; and that that star stood by itself at the edge of the canton, a little apart from the rectangle formed by the other twelve.

That this flag was carried on the Bon Homme Richard is attested by a letter of the Secretary of the Marine Committee of Congress which accompanied the flag when it was given by that committee to James Bayard Stafford in recognition of his gallant services, he having been on the Bon Homme Richard and having rescued and raised again the flag after it had been cut down during the fight. It will be recalled, however, that the Bon Homme Richard was so badly damaged that it was impossible to keep her afloat, and that Jones therefore transferred himself and his men to the conquered and captured Serapis, on which he sailed away in triumph — a unique performance. Of course he raised the Stars and Stripes above the Serapis. But as a matter of pride and sentiment he would not lower the flag of the Bon Homme Richard, but left it flying in its proper place as that vessel sank, with the bodies of her dead. Of this we have his own record:

The very last vestige mortal eyes ever saw of the Bon Homme Richard was the defiant waving of her unconquered and unstricken Flag as she went down. And as I had given them the good old ship for their sepulchre, I now bequeathed to my immortal dead the Flag they had so desperately defended, for their winding sheet.

We must assume, then, that the Flag now in cherished existence in the National Museum was another Stars and Stripes, which Jones had carried on the Bon Homme Richard and which he transferred from that vessel to the Serapis.

The Stars and Stripes was of course flying at Yorktown, when Cornwallis surrendered, and not long afterward it began to appear, in peaceful commerce, in British waters. Its first appearance in England was in a picture, painted by the American artist, John Singleton Copley. On the evening of December 5, 1782, after listening to the King's speech in Parliament announcing the preliminary treaty of peace and recognition of American independence, he went into his studio and painted the Stars and Stripes flying on a vessel which was supposed to be bearing the news of that treaty back to America. But the first actual flag was carried up the Thames to London on February 3, 1783, by Captain William Mooers, on the ship Bedford belonging to William Rotch, of Nantucket, Mass. 'This,' said a London paper of that time, 'is the first vessel which has displayed the thirteen rebellious stripes of America in any British port.'

The ship Empress of China, of New York, sailed by Captain John Green, first bore the Flag to China, entering the port of Macao on August 23, 1784. The Flag was first borne round the world by Captain John Kendrick of the Columbia and Captain Robert Gray of the Washington, who set out from Boston on September 30, 1787. Two years later, in Nootka Sound, they exchanged vessels, and Gray with the Columbia discovered the great river in Oregon to which he gave the name of his ship. Finally he reached Boston in August, 1790, completing the circumnavigation of the globe.

It was, of course, under the Stars and Stripes that the Constitutional Convention met at Philadelphia, in 1787, and formulated the fundamental law of this republic; it was under it that the States one by one ratified the Constitution and held the first election of a President and Congress; and it was under the same banner that in 1789 Washington travelled from Mount Vernon to New York, and was there inaugurated and installed as the first President of the United States. It is said

that among the decorations in the city of Philadelphia as he
passed through it there was displayed for the first time the
'American Union Jack,' consisting simply of the canton and
its stars, without the stripes, and that it contained only eleven
stars; North Carolina and Rhode Island not yet having ratified the Constitution. It appears, moreover, that some other
flags were thus and for the same reason made without the full
number of thirteen stars. Thus some are said to have been displayed with nine stars immediately after the ratification of
the Constitution by New Hampshire, the ninth State to do so,
at which time, according to its own provision, the Constitution was established in full force and effect. A little later, on
July 4, 1778, there was at Philadelphia a great celebration of
the ratification of the Constitution, and many flags with ten
stars were displayed, Virginia having also by that time given
her adherence to the instrument. Such adding of star after
star to the Flag as the remaining States ratified the Constitution may be regarded as foreshadowing the similar adding of
stars as new States in later years were created and admitted
to the Union.

CHAPTER XVI

FROM THIRTEEN TO FIFTEEN

As the Nation grew, the Flag was constrained to change. Thirteen stars and thirteen stripes were emblematic of the thirteen States. But the States were not always to remain thirteen. Fourteen years after the adoption of the Stars and Stripes the independent Republic of Vermont was annexed by Act of Congress and admitted as the fourteenth State, and in 1792 the Territory of Kentucky was also elevated to statehood. Naturally, it was felt that these new States, which in all other respects were the peers of the original thirteen, should have representation in the design of the Flag.

So it came to pass that on December 26, 1793, Stephen R. Bradley, Senator from Vermont, introduced a bill providing for the increase of the number of stars and stripes in the national standard to fifteen each. There seems to have been no debate upon this bill, and it was passed by the Senate on December 30, and the next day was reported to the House of Representatives for its action. It was promptly read a first and second time, and then laid over for further consideration.

A week later, on January 7, 1794, the Cave of the Winds was opened. The House resolved itself into Committee of the Whole, for consideration of this bill. Benjamin Goodhue, of Massachusetts, spoke first, in opposition to the bill as a 'trifling' measure, and one that might cause much future embarrassment. Once set the precedent of adding a new star and stripe for each new State, he said, we might have to keep on making such changes for a hundred years to come. In the course of fifteen years more we might have as many as twenty States, and therefore twenty stars. William Lyman, also of Massachusetts, favored the bill on the ground that Congress ought not to offend the new States. Another Massachusetts man, George Thatcher, declared that the bill was too frivolous for notice; it would set an example under which every State might change its official seal whenever a new township was created. Christopher Greenup, of Kentucky, thought it highly desirable to pass the bill and thus let the world know that we had two new States. Nathaniel Niles, of Vermont, might have been expected to urge the passage of the bill, and in fact did so, but only as the easiest way of getting rid of so insignificant a matter. Elias Boudinot, of New Jersey, formerly President of the Continental Congress, thought it desirable to please the citizens of the new States; though in the end he voted against the bill. James Madison, of Virginia, afterward President of the United States, was in favor of passing it; and so was his Virginia colleague, William R. Giles. Jeremiah Smith, of New Hampshire, perhaps still resentful because Vermont had established its independence of his State, and certainly a thrifty shipowner, closed the debate with a furious tirade against the bill and against the Senate for sending it to the House. To make such changes in all the flags on his own ships, he said, would cost him personally five hundred dollars, and would cost every vessel in the country sixty dollars!

After that, the House paused for a breathing space. The next day, January 8, however, it took the bill up again, and Benjamin Bourne, of Rhode Island, and John Watts, of New York, tried to have it referred to a special committee, or returned to the Committee of the Whole, with instructions to amend it so as to make the design of the Flag permanent and perpetual, as was 'the law of the Medes and Persians.' In this they failed, and the bill as it came from the Senate was finally passed, by a vote of 50 yeas to 42 nays. It was not, however, to go into effect until the first day of May, 1795. It is interesting to remember that this same Congress, a few weeks later in the session, provided for the building of five frigates, including the famous United States, the Constellation, and the Constitution ('Old Ironsides'), which bore that Flag of fifteen stripes and fifteen stars with heroic distinction.

So after May 1, 1795, for many memorable years the Flag of the United States displayed fifteen-fold instead of thirteen-fold symbols. That was the flag borne by our ships in the vig-

orously contested though undeclared war with France; when
Charles Cotesworth Pinckney proudly declared our policy to
be 'Millions for defence but not one cent for tribute!' It was
borne by Bainbridge and Preble and Decatur and their col-
leagues in our wars with the Barbary pirates, which European
Powers had not dared to wage, and was carried inland by an
invading expedition in North Africa, to the capture of the city
of Derne. It was the Flag which was raised at New Orleans, in
token of the sovereignty which we had acquired over the vast
Louisiana Territory, giving us forever the unchallengeable
dominance of the North American continent, and which at
the same time was carried by Lewis and Clark in their expedition across the continent to gain for us a frontage on the shore
of the Pacific Ocean. It was our Flag in the second war with
Great Britain, in Perry's victory on Lake Erie, in the midnight
battle of Lundy's Lane, in the epochal conflicts in which the
United States and the Constitution showed themselves ship for
ship superior to the oaken walls of England; it was the Flag
that waved above the dying Lawrence, as he cried to his com-
rades, 'Don't give up the ship!' — that flag of the Chesapeake
is still in existence — and it was the Flag that floated above a
rampart of cotton bales at New Orleans, when 'Old Hickory'
Jackson and his frontiersmen vanquished the veterans with
whom Wellington had conquered Napoleon. Above all, perhaps, we may recall that it was the Flag which inspired the
writing of one of the foremost of our national anthems, pre-
eminently the song of the Flag itself.

But it was also — like the Grand Union flag before it — the
Flag which brought about its own undoing. For under its
folds the domain of the United States expanded, and the
number of States was, as Benjamin Goodhue had prophesied,
from time to time increased. Tennessee was admitted to the
Union in 1796, when the new Flag was only a year old. Ohio
entered in 1803; Louisiana in 1812, after an impassioned debate, in which the right of a State to secede at will from the
Union was for the first time proclaimed on the floor of Congress, by a distinguished Representative from Massachusetts,

and was rebuked and denied by a Territorial Delegate from Mississippi! Indiana was admitted in 1816, and Mississippi in 1817; so that there were by that time five new States without representation on the Flag. Goodhue's anticipation of a total of twenty States in fifteen years had been realized in twenty-three years. Obviously, it was necessary to make another adjustment of the Flag, if it was to be an accurate symbol of the Nation.

The fact that the Flag of fifteen stars and fifteen stripes was employed in our unhappy conflict with France recalls a unique tribute which was shortly before that time paid to the American Flag by the Revolutionary Government of that country. It was in the summer of 1794, when James Monroe presented his credentials as the American Minister to the French Republic. He was publicly received by the National Convention, and was greeted with a fraternal kiss by the President of that body. A resolution was then adopted to the effect that the flags of both nations should be permanently displayed in the hall of the Convention 'as a sign of perpetual alliance and union.' A few weeks later, on September 25, Monroe presented a flag for that purpose to the President of the Convention, by the hand of Captain Joshua Barney, one of the foremost officers of the American Navy. The presentation was made at a session of the Convention, and Barney was saluted by the President with a fraternal kiss on each cheek. A resolution was then adopted making Barney an officer of the French Navy. He declined that honor at that time, because of his duties to his own country, but a little later he accepted a commission as captain and chief of division, corresponding to our rank of commodore, and held it for a few years, though without performing any services under it.

Apart from the unique circumstance of the American Flag's being thus officially displayed side by side and on an equality with the French flag in the meeting-place of the French Government, this incident is noteworthy as the first use of the fifteen-fold emblems on the Flag, seven months in advance of the lawful time for it. Monroe, in his letter to the President of the

Convention, said of the Flag, or the colors, as he called it, 'I have had them made in the form lately decreed by Congress.' But he ignored the fact that Congress had decreed the use of them in that form not immediately but 'from and after the first of May, 1795.' He thought it a graceful compliment to France, thus to give it the new Flag in advance of America's own use of it; but in fact he was giving France the Flag not in the form in which it had been allied with her own, but in the form in which, in the course of only four years, she was to regard it as a hostile emblem — when the gallant Truxtun, with the Constellation, vanquished L'Insurgente and La Vengeance, and other Americans under the same Flag scourged the ships of France wherever they could find them.

In due time a French flag was in return presented by the French Government through its Minister at Philadelphia to the American Government, and was accepted by Washington with courteous thanks, and a promise that it would be cherished among our archives. Washington at once reported the gift to the Congress, and the House of Representatives adopted suitable resolutions of appreciation. But M. Adet, the French Minister, was not satisfied with the disposition of the flag, and with amazing lack of discretion and taste wrote to the Secretary of State a long letter complaining of it and asking that it should be placed by the side of the American Flag in the halls of Congress. For this the Secretary of State, Timothy Pickering, administered to him a dignified but most significant rebuke; telling him that it was not the custom of Americans to display tokens of victories or symbols of triumphs within the meeting-places of their deliberative assemblies, and adding: 'They reverence their own customs, while they respect those of their sister republic. This, I conceive, Sir, is the way to maintain peace and good harmony between France and the United States, and not by demanding an adoption of the manners of the other; in these we must be mutually free.'

CHAPTER XVII

'THE STAR–SPANGLED BANNER'

IT was the noteworthy if not the unique distinction of the Stars and Stripes to be made, early in its history, the theme of a song which at once attained great popularity and which years afterward became the foremost of our national anthems, 'The Star-Spangled Banner.' The incident occurred near the close of our second war with Great Britain, just after that British raid upon the city of Washington which reflected gross discredit upon both the invaders and the defenders. As the British retired from that exploit, back to their ships, a number of stragglers and camp followers got drunk and misbehaved themselves so scandalously that Dr. William Beanes, of Upper Marlboro, Maryland, a sturdy and somewhat choleric old patriot, quite properly clapped some of them into jail for safe keeping. Learning of this, the British sent back a strong force and released them, and seized Dr. Beanes and took him to the fleet, with the cheerful assurance that he would presently be hanged.

Thereupon Francis Scott Key, brilliant member of a noted family, son of a gallant Revolutionary officer, and himself one of the foremost citizens of Maryland, was commissioned to go to the British fleet and seek the prisoner's release. He was accompanied on the errand by John S. Skinner, of Baltimore. The two reached the fleet on the morning of September 6, 1814, and were courteously received by the commander, the famous and formidable Vice-Admiral Sir George Cockburn, who with little hesitation ordered the release of Dr. Beanes. They were told, however, that they would all have to stay with the fleet, not as prisoners but as enforced guests, for a few days; because an important exploit was about to be undertaken, as a surprise, and the British would run no risk of having it disclosed in advance through their going ashore. The exploit was to be the storming of Fort McHenry and the capture of the city of Baltimore, in a surprise attack at night by the fleet in conjunction with a land attack by General Ross.

The fleet proceeded up the Chesapeake Bay and the Patapsco River, and made the attack as planned, on Fort McHenry, on the night of September 13; General Ross at the same time attacking at North Point. But the gallant Major George Armistead, in command of the fort, replied with a furious fire that repulsed the British fleet and caused the failure of the whole undertaking; keeping the Flag flying upon the fort through all the night of battle. The next day the British abandoned the enterprise and sailed away in defeat.

The three Americans had been on the British flagship until just before the attack, when, for safety to themselves, they were placed on the tender Minden, which kept out of the range of fire, though within plain sight of the fighting. From its deck they witnessed the conflict all night, and Key, while watching anxiously, conceived the song and wrote it upon the back of an old letter. It was because he was writing it at the very moment when the event it celebrated was being enacted that he made it so vividly realistic. 'The rockets' red glare, the bombs bursting in air,' were before his eyes as he wrote, giving ample proof 'that our Flag was still there'; proof which 'the dawn's early light' abundantly confirmed. His mention of 'the shore... where the foe's haughty host in dread silence reposes' was a reference, of course, to General Ross's army, near North Point.

The day after the battle, September 14, the British put the three men ashore, and they proceeded to Baltimore where Key revised and completed his poem and showed it to his uncle, Judge Nicholson, who was much impressed with its merits, and took it to the printing office of Benjamin Estes, where Samuel Sands put it into type and printed it on handbills for distribution on the streets. Later, on September 21, it was printed in 'The Baltimore American,' with a note telling the story of its origin but not mentioning the author's name. Charles Durang, a public singer, noticed that it would fit the air of a song which had been popular fifteen or sixteen years before, entitled 'Adams and Liberty,' an air which had first been written and used for an English drinking-song, 'To Anacreon in Heaven'; whereupon he sang it in a public restaurant next door to the Holliday Street Theatre, and after that sang it nightly in the theatre itself. It was during the brief remainder of that war immensely popular among soldiers and civilians. It was quickly conveyed to Jackson's army at New Orleans, where it was sung by the soldiers and played by the bands, both before and after the famous battle at that place. After the close of the war, the song lapsed into forget-fulness, but at the outbreak of the Civil War in 1861 it leaped again into the prominence which it has ever since enjoyed, as the favorite of American patriotic anthems.

Unlike many others, it has never been edited or changed in any way, save sometimes in a single word. The last stanza is often sung and even printed:

> Then conquer we must, for our cause it is just.

But it should be in the preferable form in which Key wrote it:

> Then conquer we must, when our cause it is just.

'The Star-Spangled Banner' — as Key felicitously named it — on Fort McHenry was of course the second form of the Flag. The 'broad stripes and bright stars' were each fifteen in number. And it is pleasant to know that the identical Flag is still in existence, piously treasured in the National Museum at Washington. It was made for the fort, or for Major Armistead, by Mrs. Mary Young Pickersgill and her two nieces, in a house on Albemarle Street, Baltimore, which is still standing. It is of heroic dimensions, measuring thirty-two feet and ten inches in length by twenty-seven feet and six inches in width. Its fifteen stars are arranged in five rows of three each, quincunx fashion. There are eleven holes in it, made by British shots. The Flag was greatly cherished by Major Armistead after the battle, and was left by him to his children. His grandson, Eben Appleton, of New York, finally placed it in the National Museum, and of all the historic flags that are there displayed, it is the most sought and most gazed upon by visitors.

CHAPTER XVIII

STANDARDIZING THE STANDARD

THE growth of the United States, as we have seen, called for another change in the Flag. After the admission of Tennessee, Ohio, Louisiana, and Indiana as States, a logical and just demand for their representation arose, and in response thereto in 1816 Peter H. Wendover, Representative in Congress from New York, moved for the appointment of a committee to consider the subject. Mr. Wendover was then serving his first term in Congress, and was not a conspicuous nor influential member. But his motion was adopted and a committee was appointed, with himself as chairman.

The first impulse of the committee was to recommend the increase of the number of stars and stripes to nineteen each, to correspond with the number of States. Happily, however, before reporting a bill to the House, the committee sought the advice of Captain Samuel Chester Reid, who had distinguished himself in 1814 by holding the British fleet at Fayal, in the Azores, with his one little privateer, the General Armstrong, long enough to give General Jackson time to prepare for its arrival at New Orleans and thus to win his brilliant victory in the battle of January 8, 1815. Captain Reid wisely advised them not to increase the number of stripes, but rather to reduce them to the former number of thirteen and to keep them forever at that number, in token of the original thirteen States. To give the additional States representation, he advised increasing the number of stars in the canton; and as doubtless other States would from time to time be added to the Union, he suggested that the proposed new law should provide for the automatic addition of a star to the Flag on every such occasion. This would 'standardize the national standard,' and establish its design for all time.

In accordance with these wise recommendations of Captain

Reid, the committee in January, 1817, reported to the House a bill providing for such changes in the Flag. But that was the 'short session,' and press of other matters caused the bill to be neglected, and it expired at the adjournment of Congress. Mr. Wendover had been reëlected, however, and upon the assembling of the new Congress in December, 1817, he renewed his former motion, the committee was reappointed, and the former report was, in substance, again presented. In speaking on the subject, he called attention to the fact that gross lack of uniformity of flags prevailed. There were at that time flying on public buildings in Washington some flags with fifteen stars and fifteen stripes, as authorized by law; some with only nine stars and nine stripes, made when only nine States had ratified the Constitution; and some with eighteen stars and eighteen stripes, made without legal authority, in recognition of new States.

Mr. Wendover, on March 24, 1818, moved for action on the bill. General Samuel Smith, of Pennsylvania, moved to postpone it indefinitely, but was defeated by an almost unanimous vote. George Poindexter, of Mississippi, who years before had called Josiah Quincy of Massachusetts to order for declaring the right of States to secede from the Union, moved to have thirteen stripes to represent the original States and seven stars to represent the new ones (Mississippi having recently entered the Union as the twentieth State), but he also was overwhelmingly beaten. Walter Folger, of Massachusetts, a grandson of Benjamin Franklin, was similarly defeated when he proposed to restore the original Flag of thirteen stars and thirteen stripes. George Robertson, of Kentucky, the eminent jurist, wanted an arbitrary number of stripes, as nine, or eleven, but could get no support. So on March 25 the bill as reported was passed by the House with only a few dissenting votes. It was promptly and unanimously passed by the Senate, and was signed by President Monroe on April 9, 1818.

This measure was entitled 'A Bill to Establish the Flag of the United States,' and provided:

That from and after the fourth day of July next, the Flag of the United States be thirteen horizontal stripes, alternate red and white; that the Union have twenty stars, white in a blue field; that on the admission of every new State into the Union, one star be added to the union of the Flag; and that such addition shall take effect on the fourth day of July next succeeding such admission.

The law did not prescribe the arrangement of the stars in the canton, and Captain Reid had, most unwisely, recommended two forms. One, for merchant vessels, the Army, federal buildings, and general use on land, was to have the twenty stars arranged to form one big star; the other, for the ships of the Navy, was to have them arranged in uniform rows. The two forms were used for a time, but the one with the big star was soon abandoned, and all flags were made alike, with the stars in rows, as they are today. Although the new Flag Law was not to go into effect until the Fourth of July, Mr. Wendover could not wait so long, but the instant his bill passed the House, without waiting for the Senate to pass and the President to sign it, he ordered a flag-maker to make him one, twenty-seven by eighteen feet in size, with the stars arranged to form one great star. He received it from New York on April 13, and on the same day had it raised on the Capitol, over the hall of the House of Representatives.

Mr. Wendover had also in mind, in agreement with Captain Reid, a so-called 'national standard,' distinguished from the Flag as the royal standard of Great Britain — after which it seems to have been patterned — is from the Union Jack and the familiar red ensign. This 'standard' was to have been divided like the British standard into four quarters. The first quarter was to be the blue canton with the twenty stars. The second was to bear the coat of arms of the United States, as shown on its Great Seal. The third was to display a female figure, representing the Goddess of Liberty; and the fourth was to be taken up by thirteen red and white stripes. This fantastic banner was to be displayed over the halls of Congress, over the White House, over navy yards and arsenals, and over any place which the President might be visiting. It does not appear that Mr. Wendover ever introduced a bill for the adoption of this 'standard,' or secured any considerable support for the idea. Beyond doubt, if he had publicly proposed it, he would have met with a defeat as decisive as was his victory with the bill for 'establishing the Flag.' The United States was not at that time minded to undertake an inept imitation of the heraldic devices of the Old Country. It was abundantly satisfied, for all uses and purposes, with the Stars and Stripes in its unheraldic simplicity, as it had been evolved contemporaneously with the evolution of the Republic itself, from the same original source, from the same causes, and by the same methods.

CHAPTER XIX

THE RISING OF THE STARS

The Flag was established by the law of 1818. Thereafter it was destined to change only as the Nation grew. But the changes were nothing but the rising of new stars into the blue field of the canton, enlarging and enriching the 'new constellation.' One indeed was already above the horizon when Mr. Wendover's bill became a law. Illinois became a State in December, 1818, and on July 4, 1819, just a year after the law went into effect, the twenty-first star was added to the Flag. Another year passed, and Independence Day of 1820 saw the stars of Alabama and Maine take their places. Then, after two years, in 1822, Missouri gained representation. Thus President Monroe, in the eight years of his Administration, saw the constellation grow from fifteen stars to twenty-four; and Benjamin Goodhue's anticipation of as many as twenty was hopelessly obsolete.

Many years then passed before more stars arose. John Quincy Adams remained for four years under a banner of twenty-four, and even the strenuous Jackson had to wait until close to the end of his eight years' reign before he could count the twenty-fifth, for Arkansas, in 1836. Van Buren began his Administration with a welcome to the star of Michigan, the twenty-sixth, in 1837. The four years of Harrison and Tyler saw no change in the Flag. But in the expansionist days of Polk new stars rose in swift and unbroken succession, one in each year. Those were the days when the United States was said to be 'bounded on the North by the Aurora Borealis, on the South by the Precession of the Equinoxes, on the East by Primæval Chaos, and on the West by the Day of Judgment!' The Fourth of July in 1845 saw conquered Florida symbolized by the twenty-seventh star; and that of 1846 saw the Lone Star of Texas enter the canton as the twenty-eighth. Then, to keep the numerical balance true between the North and South, there followed Iowa in 1847 and Wisconsin in 1848. Thus the original thirteen had grown to thirty; and beyond the western horizon other stars were waiting to rise in the reverse of nature's order.

It was while Millard Fillmore was serving out Taylor's unfinished term that California, in 1851, added her golden star. Five years before it had been hoped and expected that Texas would divide her star into five, but she chose to remain, after her entry into the Union, what she had been in her brief independence, the 'Lone Star State.' So it had been thought that California would provide two stars, but she declined to do so and contented herself with one, the thirty-first. The Administration of Pierce was barren. But that of Buchanan saw Minnesota enter the Union and add her star in 1858, and far-off Oregon also contribute to the Flag in 1859. Thus it was a Flag of thirty-three stars at the crisis when secession sought to despoil the constellation for the creation of a rival Southern Cross.

Lincoln, however, refused to admit that any stars had been removed, either to form another constellation or to 'darkle in the trackless void'; and he retained all the thirty-three. More, he added others. That of oppressed and martyred Kansas, long unjustly excluded, was welcomed in 1861; and it was followed two years later by that of West Virginia, the first and only State ever formed by the rending asunder of one already existing. Then, while Andrew Johnson was filling out Lincoln's uncompleted second term, there arose in our firmament the stars of Nevada in 1865 and Nebraska in 1867, making a total of thirty-seven.

It was one of Fate's ironies that Grant, who had been the foremost militant protagonist in retaining would-be wandering stars in the Flag, should during his eight years as President see no new star added. He did see a new State, Colorado, admitted to the Union in 1876, but its star did not appear in the Flag until 1877. Thus in a dual sense that is the 'Centennial State,' entering the Union in the one hundredth year of

American Independence, and winning representation in the Flag in the centennial year of the Stars and Stripes.

Then came the longest interval save one in the history of the Flag's starry growth. There had been a gap of fourteen years between the twenty-fourth star, Missouri, in 1822, and the twenty-fifth, Arkansas, in 1836. Thirteen years similarly elapsed between Colorado in 1877 and the next addition to the Flag, in 1890. But then the long delay was amply atoned for in the greatest numerical increase of the constellation ever known in a single year. Before that time, indeed, all stars had come in singly, save for the one doublet of Alabama and Maine, just seventy years before. On the Fourth of July, 1890, President Harrison had the proud and unique privilege of saluting no fewer than five new stars, bringing the total to forty-three, or four more than three times the original number. These States were North Dakota, South Dakota, Montana, Washington, and Idaho; and the last-named won its place in the Flag that year by a margin of less than twenty-four hours. For Idaho was admitted to the Union on the third of July, and thus under the law was entitled to a star in the Flag on the following day. Nor did this unexampled achievement of five stars in one year complete Harrison's record; for the very next year, 1891, the star of Wyoming was added to the Flag. Thus in his four years six stars entered the constellation; a greater number than is credited to any other President, save only James Monroe.

The second Administration of Grover Cleveland saw the star of Utah, the forty-fifth, take its place in the Flag. Then, despite the so-called era of expansion and imperialism — which was nothing but traditional Americanism — a dozen years passed before another star arose; that of Oklahoma, in 1908, in the second Administration of Theodore Roosevelt. Then finally the last available Territory for statehood was used by William Howard Taft, who in 1912 saluted the risen stars of New Mexico and Arizona, the forty-seventh and forty-eighth of the 'new' constellation which was a hundred and thirty-five years old. We say that this was the last available Territory, because many years before the Government had strongly committed itself to the principle that all States of this Union must consist of contiguous Continental territory, and never include detached and outlying lands. If that principle shall be maintained, then, barring the possible but most improbable contingency of the division of some existing State, the Stars and Stripes is now at last 'established' in a dual sense, in the general design and in the number of its stars as well as of its stripes.

Because of the varying number of them, and for other reasons including personal taste or caprice, the stars in the Union were formerly arranged in a diversity of ways. In the flag carried by John Paul Jones on the Bon Homme Richard they were in parallel rows and parallel columns, as at present. In the Fort McHenry Flag which inspired Key to write 'The Star-Spangled Banner,' they were in quincunx order, and for some years that arrangement was officially prescribed. But with the filling of the Union with forty-eight stars, on October 26, 1912, an Executive Order of President Taft directed that they should thereafter be placed in six horizontal rows of eight stars each, making eight parallel columns of six stars each.

In fact, of course, all the stars, whatever their place in the canton, are of equal dignity, worth, and significance, as are the States themselves which the stars represent. In theory and in sentiment each State has its own individual star in the Flag, according to the chronological order in which the States adopted the Constitution and entered the Union. Thus beginning with the first row and reading from left to right, as in reading a book, the first star, in the upper left hand corner of the canton, is that of Delaware, the first of all States to ratify the Constitution; and the other stars in that row are (2) Pennsylvania, (3) New Jersey, (4) Georgia, (5) Connecticut, (6) Massachusetts, (7) Maryland, and (8) South Carolina. The second row begins at the left with (9) New Hampshire, followed by (10) Virginia, (11) New York, (12) North Carolina, and (13) Rhode Island, thus completing the original thirteen, with (14) Vermont, (15) Kentucky, and (16) Tennessee to fill out that line. The third line runs: (17) Ohio, (18) Louisiana, (19) Indiana, (20) Mississippi, (21) Illinois, (22) Alabama, (23) Maine, and (24) Missouri; the fourth line: (25) Arkansas, (26) Michigan, (27) Florida, (28) Texas, (29) Iowa, (30) Wisconsin, (31) California, and (32), Minnesota; the fifth line: (33) Oregon, (34) Kansas, (35) West Virginia, (36) Nevada, (37) Nebraska, (38) Colorado, (39) North Dakota, and (40) South Dakota; and the sixth line: (41) Montana, (42) Washington, (43) Idaho, (44) Wyoming, (45) Utah, (46) Oklahoma, (47) New Mexico, and (48) Arizona.

CHAPTER XX

PIONEERS

WE have already heard of the first carrying of the Stars and
Stripes around the world. That historic cruise was made
around Cape Horn, and not until many years later was the
Flag borne through the Straits of Magellan, on the route made
memorable in American naval annals by the voyage of the
Oregon at the beginning of our war with Spain in 1898. The
first American merchant vessel to pass through the Straits
seems to have been the Endeavor, of Salem, Massachusetts,
commanded by David Elwell, in 1824; while the first of our
Navy to do so was the schooner Shark, commanded by Lieutenant A. Bigelow, in 1839.

This last-named year saw, also, another and still more
memorable adventure under the Stars and Stripes. This was
the Antarctic exploring expedition sent out by the United
States Navy under the command of Charles Wilkes, a nephew
of the famous English politician and friend of America, John
Wilkes. This expedition made important researches, and discovered the region known as Wilkes Land, directly south of
Australia. One of its vessels, the little New York pilot boat
Flying Fish, under Lieutenant William W. Walker, pene-
trated to Latitude 70° 14′ South, the farthest south that had
then ever been reached, save by the Weddell expedition. Attempts were made by British explorers and geographers to
discredit Wilkes's reports, especially after he had personally
incurred much odium in Great Britain by his intrepid but
ill-advised act in our Civil War, when with his ship the San
Jacinto he stopped the British mail steamer Trent and took
from it two Confederate envoys, Messrs. Slidell and Mason;
and for years his name was not printed on British maps of the
Antarctic regions. In later times, however, his achievements
have been fully and handsomely recognized, and he is credited

with having borne the Stars and Stripes first of all flags to that part of the Antarctic Continent.

The American Flag was also a still more noteworthy pioneer in the 'Sahara of the North.' After the disappearance of the British explorer, Sir John Franklin, on his quest for the North west Passage, Henry Grinnell, of New York, generously fitted out an expedition to search for him, and in 1850 it went to the Arctic regions, under the command of Lieutenant Edwin J. De Haven, of the United States Navy. Its errand was fruit less, so far as finding Franklin or traces of him was concerned and a little later Mr. Grinnell sent another expedition thither under the direction of Dr. Elisha Kent Kane. It did not find Franklin, but it carried the Stars and Stripes farther north than any other flag had ever been. That was in 1854. Seven years later, Dr. I. I. Hayes, who had been a member of Kane' expedition, went thither again, and made another 'farthest north' record; planting at the extreme point reached a small Stars and Stripes that had been carried to the Antarctic in Wilkes's expedition.

A third time the American Flag went nearer than any other to the North Pole, in 1883, when it was borne thither by Messrs. Brainard and Lockwood, members of the scientific research expedition led by Lieutenant — afterward General —A. W. Greely. This record was exceeded afterward by Dr Frithiof Nansen and others, but American supremacy in the Arctic was triumphantly established for all time on April 6 1909, when after several unsuccessful attempts Commander Robert E. Peary, U.S.N., first of all men reached the North Pole and planted there the Stars and Stripes — 'on the Top of the World.'

Another epochal leadership of the Stars and Stripes was recorded in 1852–54, when Commodore Matthew Calbraith Perry, younger brother of the hero of the Battle of Lake Erie carried the Flag into the harbor of Yeddo, Japan, and effected the 'opening' of that hermit empire to rational intercourse with the civilized world. In that achievement the Flag was in a transcendent sense and degree the pioneer in beginning new chapter of inestimable importance in the history of man-kind; an achievement second in importance, we might say, only to that of the flag of Leon and Castile in leading the way to the European colonization of the American continents.

Arduous and romantic beyond description were two other adventures of the Flag, in the hands of a naturalized American citizen, a civilian, Henry Morton Stanley; not in the sterile wastes of the Polar wilderness of ice, but in the torrid jungles of Equatorial Africa. It was in 1871 that Mr. Stanley pene-trated to Ujiji, in the heart of the Dark Continent, and there found the illustrious explorer and missionary, David Living-stone, who had for years been lost to the world. There have been few more interesting scenes than that of the meeting of the two white men, amid a multitude of black natives, in the African wilderness, when Stanley, carrying the Stars and Stripes in one hand and raising his hat with the other, in-quired: 'Doctor Livingstone, I presume?' Three years later, Stanley went to Africa again, and made his way from the East Coast to the Great Lakes, thence to the upper reaches of the Congo, and so down that mighty river to its mouth. Thus the Stars and Stripes was the first flag ever to be borne clear across the Equatorial regions of the Dark Continent, from the Indian Ocean to the Atlantic; the first to follow the thitherto unknown course of the Congo; and the pioneer in opening the way for the creation of the Congo Free State.

We might tell many chapters more of the achievements of those who carried the Stars and Stripes; of its being planted in peace, in 1867, upon the vast Arctic and sub-Arctic realm of Alaska; and also in 1898 upon 'summer isles of Eden, lying in dark purple spheres of sea,' in the mid-Pacific; of its liberation of the 'Pearl of the Antilles' from an odious yoke, and of its sovereignty over some of the last remnants of Spain's ancient empire in both hemispheres; of its having been borne where Balboa bore the flag of Spain and its thus fulfilling the world's age-long desire in the completion of the Isthmian waterway which Columbus sought and Cortez planned; of its having blazed the way to victory and peace in that World War which made of half the European Continent a Field of Armageddon. But thus to tell the history of the Stars and Stripes would largely be to tell the history of the world. For now, and for more than a century, have been realized the words of its most illustrious eulogist, that 'the gorgeous ensign of the Republic' is indeed 'known and honored throughout the earth,' and that 'its ample folds float over the sea and over the land and in every wind under the whole heavens.'

The President's Flag

Marine Corps
Standard

Coast Guard Ensign

Red Cross and
Hospital Flag

Confederate 'Stars and
Bars'

Confederate Battle Flag

CHAPTER XXI

FLAGS OF THE 'LOST CAUSE'

IT would be unfitting to close a history of the American Flag without some mention of the banners which for four years were the cherished emblems of one-third of the Nation. These were four in number, though the longest-lived and best beloved of them had no official sanction.

The first of the four was adopted by the Convention of the Confederate States of America at Montgomery, Alabama, on March 4, 1861; the very day on which Abraham Lincoln became President of the United States, and was thus pledged to prevent or to destroy the sovereignty which that flag purported to represent. It was designed by Major Orren Randolph Smith of Louisburg, North Carolina, and was reported to the Convention by William Porcher Miles, the eminent educator, President of North Carolina College, who frankly confessed that there had been a strong desire to retain in it a suggestion of the Stars and Stripes. In fact there was much more than a suggestion; there was a striking likeness.

The 'Stars and Bars,' as this flag was commonly called at the North more than at the South, retained the same colors as those of the Stars and Stripes, used in the same way. The canton was blue, with a circle of seven white stars, to be increased to correspond with the number of the Confederate States, and the field was covered with three broad stripes, or 'bars,' the top and bottom red and the middle white. The resemblance to the Stars and Stripes was so great as not infrequently to cause one to be mistaken for the other, especially amid the smoke and dust of battle, the very occasion when such a mistake was most mischievous. In consequence there was much unfavorable criticism of it, and for use in battle another flag was made in its stead.

The latter, never officially sanctioned by the Confederate Government, was designed by William Porcher Miles and was his personal choice for the official flag of the Confederacy. But as it was first used by General Pierre G. T. Beauregard, it was often called 'Beauregard's battle flag,' and also the 'Battle Flag of the Confederacy'; and the 'Southern Cross.' It consisted of a red field spanned by a blue Saint Andrew's Cross edged with white and bearing along its arms thirteen white stars, for by that time there were thirteen States claimed by the Confederacy, though in fact only eleven actually seceded from the Union, the Border States of Kentucky and Missouri declaring themselves 'neutral.' This 'battle flag' was impressive and effective, and impossible to mistake for the Stars and Stripes, and it enjoyed during the Civil War unbounded popularity and affection throughout the South.

The 'Stars and Bars,' despite dissatisfaction and unfavorable comment, remained the official flag of the Confederate States for more than two years, or until May 1, 1863. Then the Congress at Richmond adopted a substitute which, while amending some errors, fell into others equally deplorable. This second Confederate flag, which by some of its advocates was called the 'White Man's Flag,' consisted of a plain white field, with Beauregard's battle flag as a canton. But the length of the field was made twice its width, an awkward and inartistic shape; and the battle flag was shortened into a square for the canton, and made two-thirds of the width of the field, thus grossly disproportionate, being too short for the length and too broad for the width of the flag. Moreover, the flag bore too great a resemblance to the White Ensign of the British Navy, while the preponderance of the white field might cause it to be mistaken for a flag of truce. So, although officially adopted and promulgated, it was never popular, but continued, like its predecessor, to yield precedence in action to the battle flag.

It continued to be the official flag of the Confederacy, however, for nearly two years, until February 4, 1865. Then, with the Confederacy itself fast crumbling into ruin, the Congress adopted its third official flag. This was a modification of the second, and in some respects was a marked improvement on it. The dimensions were altered, so as to make the width two-thirds instead of only one-half the length. The battle flag canton, too, was made horizontally oblong instead of square. These were admirable changes, from the artistic point of view, giving the flag correct and graceful proportions. Unfortunately, however, to lessen its likeness to a flag of truce, a broad vertical stripe of red was placed across its outer end, equal in width to the remaining portion of the white field, thus reducing the latter to the form of a huge capital letter L, with the canton lying in the angle of its arms. Probably this would have prevented it from being mistaken for a flag of truce. But it certainly made it one of the most inartistic of flags, and would have debarred it from popular favor, even had time permitted it to be brought into general use.

But time did not permit it. This flag was never made in considerable numbers, but remained existent chiefly on paper. For just two months and five days after its adoption by the Congress at Richmond, Lee surrendered at Appomattox, and the Confederacy and its flags passed into history. It was under the battle flag, moreover, that Lee surrendered; the flag that had been carried through many a desperate conflict, from Galveston to Gettysburg, from Donelson to Mobile Bay. More than all the three Congressionally ordained and official flags, this unofficial standard, ordained by the strenuous decrees of mortal strife, stood and must always stand as the supreme ensign of the Confederate States of America.

Nor could anything be more fitting. For from beginning to end the life of the Confederacy was a life of battle. It began with the beginning of a war and ended with the ending of that war. Its proper emblem was a battle flag. Nor can the perceptive vision fail to behold a singular significance, witting or unwitting, in the design of that standard. It retained the colors of the Stars and Stripes, even as the Stars and Stripes had retained those of the 'Meteor Flag of England,' thus proclaiming itself to be in the authentic line of descent. It retained, too, the characteristic feature of the Stars and Stripes, in having one star for each of the States. It used, moreover, as stars, not the wavy-pointed nor the six-pointed stars of heraldry, but the five-pointed spur-rowels which were first thus used and thus called in the Stars and Stripes. And finally, by some motive none the less inspired because unconscious and unintended, it harked back to the old King's Colors of Colonial days and combined its saltire of Saint Andrew with the thirteen stars of America's New Constellation. Flag of the Lost Cause, it is one of the most illuminating and imperishable emblems in American history.

CHAPTER XXII

SALUTE!

'I PLEDGE allegiance to the Flag of the United States and to the Republic for which it stands: One nation, indivisible, with liberty and justice for all!'

Millions of American children, standing at 'Attention!' and with hands raised in formal salute, daily repeat that pledge to a Flag which stands before them and which flies upon the building in which they are assembled. The first step toward such observance in public schools was taken away back in May, 1812, at Catamount Hill, Colrain, Massachusetts, at not a 'little red schoolhouse,' but one of logs with bark instead of paint. It was at the beginning of a war that was so unpopular in that part of the country that many people were inclined to revolt against the Government for waging it. But a number of families at Catamount Hill were aggressively loyal, and they signified that fact by raising the Flag above the local school; an event commemorated by an inscription on a huge stone on the site of the little log house.

It does not appear that the example was widely followed, and the practice lapsed and was all but forgotten. But when the Civil War began in 1861, it was revived by the raising of a Flag on the high school in New Bedford, Massachusetts, and thence quickly spread throughout all the Northern States. Later such use of the Flag on all public schoolhouses when school is in session was made a legal requirement in most of the States.

The formal saluting of the Flag and repetition of the pledge must be credited largely to the efforts of James B. Upham, a publisher of Boston, who in 1888 began arousing public thought upon the subject of inspiring and cultivating patriotism by placing a National Flag in and upon every schoolhouse. In 1891 he urged that the four-hundredth anniversary of the Columbian discovery of America, in October, 1892, be commemorated in the schools with flag-raisings and salutes. This plan was adopted by the National Education Association, and was carried out with great success. It was on that occasion that the Pledge to the Flag, almost precisely as now used, was first given. It had been drafted by Mr. Upham, and in the generation since has been repeated by the lips and impressed upon the minds and hearts of uncounted millions of American youths.

It was in the early days of the Civil War that the Stars and Stripes began to be generally displayed upon and in the churches of the land. Some churches raised the Flag on their spires or towers, or on staffs set in the ground of the churchyard. Others placed it within, near the altar or the pulpit, and this latter practice, continued in time of peace, has now become common to probably a majority of churches.

The anniversary of the adoption of the Stars and Stripes, June 14, has not been made a nation-wide legal holiday, but in late years has increasingly been regarded as a day for suitable commemoration, in schools, in churches, and by social and patriotic organizations; and for a general display of the Flag by all citizens; such observance being recommended by the Governors of States in public proclamations. The initiative in this most commendable practice appears to have been taken by Jonathan Flynt Morris, of Hartford, Connecticut, in the spring of 1861. Under the stress and urge of the Civil War such as caused the display of the Flag at schools and churches, he asked Charles Dudley Warner, one of the editors of 'The Hartford Courant,' to write in that paper an editorial suggesting the celebration of Flag Day. Warner complied to so good effect that the day was that year generally observed throughout that State, though, strangely enough, on June 8 instead of 14. The next important step was taken in 1877, when the one hundredth anniversary of the adoption of the Stars and Stripes was nationally commemorated, on June 14. Nothing more was done toward establishing yearly observance, however, until 1892. Then LeRoy Van Horn, a Civil War veteran, of Chicago, took the matter up, presumably through the inspiration of Mr. Upham's publication already mentioned. At any rate, he anticipated the nation-wide school celebration of October 12, 1892 — Columbus Day, then first proclaimed a public holiday — by assembling a great multitude of school children in one of the parks of Chicago on June 14, and holding exercises of flag-raising, saluting, singing, and speaking in honor of the Stars and Stripes. In this movement, so well begun, others interested themselves, notably Dr. B. J. Cigrand, George Balch, and George A. Cantine. In 1897 the Governor of New York first issued a proclamation for observance of the day, and ordered a display of the Flag on all public buildings; and in 1917, because of America's entry into the World War, the President of the United States proclaimed June 14, for that occasion only, a public holiday throughout the Nation.

The World War gave another great impetus to the greater honoring of the Flag. It was then that men learned always to uncover their heads or to stand at 'Salute!' whenever the Flag passed by. It was then that more scrupulous attention was given to the right usage of the Flag; to the manner of raising it and lowering it; to its proper position when hung elsewhere than on a staff. It was then that people were made to realize that the Flag is a flag and nothing else, and should always be thus used, and not as a decoration, festooned or gathered into a rosette, nor as a table cover or other article of utility. It was then that they appreciated the importance, when it was being raised or lowered, of bearing it up in their hands and never letting it trail upon the ground.

The abuse and actual desecration of the Flag, whether thoughtless or purposed, was in former years so common as to move the Daughters of the American Revolution to seek national legislation for the abatement of the evil. One of the early acts of that patriotic society, in 1896, was to cause the introduction of a bill in the Congress forbidding under penalty the placing upon or attaching to the Flag any political or commercial inscription or device, or the mutilating of it in any way. Much popular support for this measure was shown, through the leadership of the Daughters of the American Revolution, but it was impossible to get it beyond the custody of a Congressional committee. The efforts of the Daughters were not, however, in vain; for as a result of the popular sentiment thus aroused, individual States enacted laws similar to that which had been asked of the Congress, and Justice Harlan, of the Supreme Court of the United States, officially expressed the opinion that it was the right and duty of every State to enact adequate legislation for the protection of the national ensign. Moreover, the Congress in 1905 forbade the registering of any trademark which included in its design the Flag, the coat of arms or other insignia of the United States; and in 1917 it enacted just such a law as the Daughters had originally sought for the protection of the Flag from desecration, applicable, however, only to the District of Columbia.

A final act of supreme importance in the inculcation of a proper regard for and treatment of the Flag, by civilians — the Army and Navy having long had their official codes — was performed on Flag Day, June 14, 1923. There then met at Washington a national convention of representatives of sixty-eight civic, patriotic, and educational organizations, comprising more than five million members, and also representatives of the Army and Navy in an advisory capacity. This gathering was convoked by the American Legion, and was presided over by the head of its National Americanization Commission, Garland W. Powell. Its sessions, which lasted two days, were held in Memorial Continental Hall, the home of the Daughters of the American Revolution, and the first was formally opened by the President of the United States, Warren G. Harding. The result was the drafting and adoption of a comprehensive code of Flag etiquette, and the creation of a permanent committee of six, known as the Committee of the National Flag Conference on Education in the Correct Use of the Flag. The code, which appears in full in the appendix of this volume, was drafted by a committee consisting of Gridley Adams, of the Sons of Veterans; Mrs. Anthony Wayne Cook, of the Daughters of the American Revolution;

Major O. C. Luxford, of the Sons of the American Revolution; B. S. Martin, of the Boy Scouts of America; Mrs. Henry Osgood Holland, of the National Congress of Mothers; John L. Riley, of the American Legion; Lieutenant-Colonel H. S. Herrick, of the American Legion; Mrs. Livingston Rowe Schuyler, of the United Daughters of the Confederacy; and Captain Chester Wells of the United States Navy and Captain George M. Chandler of the United States Army.

The code thus prepared, adopted, and promulgated has not the legal force of a legislative enactment. But it has the greater moral force of the expressed will of a patriotic people, intent upon defending, cherishing, and honoring their self-chosen symbol of their law and their liberty, their power and their sovereignty, their justice and their sacred honor. Born in the war which made us independent, the Flag was raised above a public school and received its lyric glorification in the war which — as our foeman confessed — made us formidable; it entered into all our schools and churches and into our national life as never before in the war which for all time confirmed our national unity; and finally in the World War it attained the fulness of its estate as the visible emblem of the body, the mind, and the soul of the American nation.

The theme of the loftiest flights of poets and orators innumerable, volumes might be filled with the tributes that have been paid to it, of all of which it is abundantly worthy. Three only may here be given, standing 'first among equals' in their classic felicity. One is the tremendous climax of what by common consent is held the greatest Senatorial oration ever delivered upon the American continent, Daniel Webster's reply to Robert Y. Hayne:

When my eyes shall turn to behold, for the last time, the sun in heaven, may I not see him shining on the broken and dishonored fragments of a once glorious Union; on States dissevered, discordant, belligerent; on a land rent with civil feuds, or drenched, it may be, in fraternal blood. Let their last feeble and lingering glance rather behold the gorgeous ensign of the Republic, now known and honored throughout the earth, still full high advanced, its arms and trophies streaming in their original lustre, not a stripe erased or polluted, not a single star obscured, bearing for its motto no such miserable interrogatory as *What is all this worth?* nor those other words of delusion and folly, *Liberty first, and Union afterwards;* but everywhere spread all over in characters of living light, blazing on all its ample folds as they float over the sea and over the land, and in every wind under the whole heavens, that other sentiment, dear to every true American heart, 'LIBERTY AND UNION, NOW AND FOREVER, ONE AND INSEPARABLE!'

The second is found in the address of Robert C. Winthrop, in October, 1861, on the occasion of the marching of troops to the front in the Civil War:

The national ensign, pure and simple ... Behold it! Listen to it! Every star has a tongue. Every stripe is articulate. There is no language nor speech where their voices are not heard. There is magic in the web of it. It has an answer for every question. It has a solution for every doubt and every perplexity. It has a word of good cheer for every hour of gloom or of despondency. Behold it! Listen to it! It speaks of earlier and of later struggles. It speaks of heroes and patriots among the living and among the dead. But before and above all other associations and memories, whether of glorious men or glorious deeds or glorious places, its voice is ever of Union and Liberty, of the Constitution and the Laws!

The third, worn, hackneyed, threadbare, as familiar to us as the Flag itself, is the 'Ode' of Joseph Rodman Drake, written in May, 1819, a year after the Flag had been 'established' in its permanent form. It would be superfluous to recall its virile verses here in full; but we may well commiserate the man who, however far removed in years from his school-day declamation of them, does not yet thrill with nameless, irrepressible emotion as he once more repeats:

> Flag of the free heart's hope and home,
>   By angel hands to valor given,
> Thy stars have lit the welkin dome,
>   And all thy hues were born in Heaven!
> Forever float that standard sheet!
>   Where breathes the foe but falls before us,
> With Freedom's soil beneath our feet,
>   And Freedom's banner streaming o'er us!

APPENDIX

APPENDIX I

SPECIAL AMERICAN FLAGS

UNLIKE some other countries, which have national, naval, merchant, and other flags of differing designs, America has only the one Flag, the Stars and Stripes, and its Union, for all purposes; official and civilian, army, navy, and mercantile marine. It has, however, many special flags, for individual officials and branches of the public service.

The Commission Pennant of the Navy is a flag ten times as long as it is wide, and tapering from its greatest width, at the staff, to a point, or rather two points, at the other end. About two-fifths of it, at the broad end, is blue with thirteen stars in a single row, and the remainder is divided into two narrow stripes, the upper red and the lower white.

The President's flag has a dark blue field, with a white star in each corner and the President's seal in the centre.

The flag of the Secretary of State is dark blue, with the obverse of the Great Seal of the United States in the centre, with a white star at each side of it.

The flag of the Secretary of the Treasury is dark blue, with an escutcheon in the centre with two crossed anchors, a balance, and a key, surrounded by thirteen white stars in a circle. That of the Assistant Secretary is the same with the colors reversed.

The flag of the Secretary of War is red, with the obverse of the Great Seal in the centre and a white star in each of the four corners. That of the Assistant Secretary is the same with the colors reversed.

The flag of the Secretary of the Navy is dark blue, with an upright white anchor in the centre and a white star in each corner. That of the Assistant Secretary is the same, with the colors reversed.

The flag of the Secretary of the Interior consists of three stripes of equal width, the top and bottom light blue and the middle white, with the seal of the Department in the centre, and above it three and below it four white stars.

The flag of the Secretary of Commerce is dark blue, with a white shield in the centre, bearing in dark blue a ship on its upper and a lighthouse on its lower part, and with a white star at each corner. That of the Assistant Secretary is the same, with the colors reversed.

The flag of the Secretary of Labor is white, with the seal of the Department at the centre, its escutcheon red and gold, and with a dark blue star at each corner. The flag of the Immigration Service of that Department is tapering and swallow-tailed, white with a narrow dark blue stripe at top and bottom, with the red and gold escutcheon in the centre, with the red letters U.S.I.S.

The Revenue or Custom House flag of the Treasury Department was adopted in 1799, when there were sixteen States, and it consists of sixteen perpendicular red and white stripes, beginning with a red stripe next the staff, and with a white canton bearing the arms of the United States, in blue, underneath an arch of thirteen blue stars. The Coast Guard has this same flag for its ensign, with the addition of its escutcheon on the thirteenth (a red) stripe. The standard of the Coast Guard is white, with the arms of the United States in blue in the centre; above them an arch of thirteen stars and over it the legend 'United States Coast Guard,' and below the arms the motto *Semper Paratus* and the date 1790. There are various other flags for the Commandant and the force, division, and other Commanders of the Coast Guard.

The Public Health Service has for the Surgeon-General a dark blue flag with an anchor and a caduceus crossed, in white, at the centre; and a Public Health flag of yellow with the same design in dark blue.

The Department of Commerce has for the Bureau of Navigation a dark blue flag with a white ship on a red disc in the centre; for the Commissioner of Navigation a dark blue flag with a white ship; for the Coast and Geodetic Survey a dark blue flag with a red triangle on a white disc, and for its director a dark blue flag with a white triangle; for the Bureau of Fisheries a dark blue flag with a white fish in a red diamond, and for its Commissioner the same without the red diamond; for the Bureau of Lighthouses a triangular flag of white, with a red border and a blue lighthouse on the white; for the Commissioner of Lighthouses an oblong flag of dark blue with a blue lighthouse in a white triangle; and for the Inspector of Lighthouses a white flag with dark blue border and dark blue lighthouse.

The War Department has an Engineer's flag, red, with a white armory building; a Transport flag with red and blue triangles and a diagonal white stripe between them, and on the white a blue wheel surmounted by an eagle and crossed by sword and key; and a Quartermaster's pennant with a red triangle above and a blue triangle below, and between them a white diamond with the wheel and eagle as on the Transport flag.

The Marine Corps has various flags, the standard being dark blue, with a white disc in the centre representing the Western Hemisphere, with the American Continents in gold, crossed by an anchor, surmounted by an eagle, and partly surrounded by laurels.

The flag of an Admiral is dark blue with four white stars, of a Vice-Admiral the same with three stars, of a Rear-Admiral the same with two stars, and of a Commodore the same but swallow-tailed and with one star. Junior officers of these ranks have red flags instead of blue. The merchant marine of the Naval Reserve has a dark blue flag, swallow-tailed, with an escutcheon with crossed anchors surmounted by an eagle. The Naval Militia's flag is dark blue with a blue anchor in a yellow diamond.

The Consular flag is dark blue with a large letter C surrounded by a circle of thirteen stars, all white, in the centre.

The Army, beside the Stars and Stripes, is provided with numerous regimental and other flags and guidons. There are also boat flags for the use of Army officers when making official visits to vessels of the Navy. These are red, with white stars indicating the rank of the officer — four for a General, three for a Lieutenant-General, two for a Major-General, and one for a Brigadier-General. The Red Cross or Hospital flag is white with a large red Cross in the centre of the pattern known as the Geneva Cross, with four broad arms of equal length.

The Church flag is a long, narrow triangle of white, bearing a large blue Cross placed lengthwise upon the field, its head toward the staff. This is displayed during the hours of divine worship, flying above the Stars and Stripes, and is the only flag ever placed above the national ensign.

APPENDIX II

THE CODE OF THE FLAG

THE Code of the Flag, for observance by civilians, adopted by the National Flag Conference at Washington on June 14–15, 1923, is as follows:

The Flag of the United States symbolized that freedom, equality, justice and humanity for which our forefathers sacrificed their lives and personal fortunes. To-day this Flag represents a nation of over 100,000,000 free people, its Constitution and institutions, its achievements, and aspirations.

There are certain fundamental rules of heraldry which, if understood generally, would indicate the proper method of displaying the Flag. The matter becomes a very simple one if it is kept in mind that the national Flag represents the living country and is itself considered as a living thing. The Union of the Flag is the honor point; the right arm is the sword arm and therefore the point of danger and hence the place of honor.

DESCRIPTION OF FLAG

The Flag of the United States has thirteen horizontal stripes — seven red and six white — the red and white stripes alternating, and a union which consists of white stars of five points on a blue field placed in the upper quarter next the staff and extending to the lower edge of the fourth red stripe from the top. The number of stars is the same as the number of States in the Union. The canton or union now contains forty-eight stars, arranged in six horizontal and eight vertical rows, each star with one point upward. On the admission of a state into the Union a star will be added to the union of the flag, and such addition will take effect on the fourth day of July next succeeding such admission. The proportions of the Flag, as prescribed by Executive Order of President Taft, October 29, 1912, are as follows:

Hoist (width) of flag	1.
Fly (length) of flag	1.9.
Hoist (width) of union	7.13.
Fly (length) of union	0.76.
Width of each stripe	1.13.
Diameter of star	0.0616.

MANNER OF DISPLAYING FLAG

1. The Flag should be displayed from sunrise to sunset only or between such source as designated by proper authority on national and state holidays, and on historic and special occasions. The Flag should always be hoisted briskly and lowered slowly and ceremoniously.

2. When carried in a procession with another flag or flags the place of the Flag of the United States is on the right, i.e., the Flag's own right, or when there is a line of other flags the Flag of the United States may be in front of the center of that line.

3. When displayed with another flag, against a wall from crossed staffs, the Flag of the United States should be on the right, the Flag's own right, and its staff should be in front of the staff of the other flag.

4. When a number of flags are grouped and displayed from staffs the Flags of the United States should be in the center or at the highest point of the group.

5. When flags of states or cities or pennants of societies are flown on the same halyard with the Flag of the United States the Flag of the United States must always be at the peak. When flown from adjacent staffs the Flag of the United States should be hoisted first. No flag or pennant should be placed above or to the right of the Flag of the United States.

6. When the flags of two or more nations are to be displayed they should be flown from separate staffs of the same height and the flags should be of equal size. (International usage forbids the display of the flag of one nation above that of any other nation in time of peace.)

7. When the Flag is displayed from a staff projecting horizontally or at an angle from the windowsill, balcony or front of building, the union of the Flag should go clear to the head of the staff unless the Flag is at half-staff.

8. When the Flag of the United States is displayed other than flown from a staff it should be displayed flat, whether indoors or out. When displayed either horizontally or vertically against a wall the union should be uppermost and at the Flag's right; that is, to the observer's left. When displayed in a window it should be displayed the same way; that is, with the union or blue field to the left of the observer in the street. When festoons or drapings of blue, white and red are desired, bunting should be used, but never the Flag.

9. When displayed over the middle of the street, as between buildings, the Flag of the United States should be suspended vertically with the union to the north in an east and west street or to the east in a north and south street.

10. When used on a speaker's platform the Flag should be displayed above and behind the speaker. It should never be used to cover the speaker's desk nor drape over the front of the platform. If flown from a staff it should be on the speaker's right.

11. When used in unveiling a statue or monument the Flag should not be allowed to fall to the ground, but should be carried aloft to wave out, forming a distinctive feature during the remainder of the ceremony.

12. When flown at half-staff the Flag is first hoisted briskly to the peak and then lowered to the half-staff position, but before lowering the Flag for the day it is raised again to the peak. On Memorial Day, May 30, the Flag is displayed at half-staff from sunrise until noon and at full staff from noon until sunset; for the Nation lives and the Flag is the symbol of the living Nation.

13. When used to cover a casket the Flag should be placed so that the union is at the head and over the left shoulder. The Flag should not be lowered into the grave nor allowed to touch the ground. The casket should be carried feet first.

14. When the Flag is displayed in church it should be from a staff placed on the congregation's right as they face the clergyman, with the service flag, State flag or other flag on the left wall. If in the chancel the Flag of the United States should be placed on the clergyman's right as he faces the congregation.

15. When the Flag is in such a condition that it is no longer a fitting emblem for display it should not be cast aside or used in any way that might be viewed as disrespectful to the national colors, but should be destroyed as a whole, privately, preferably by burning or by some other method in harmony with the reverence and respect we owe to the emblem representing our country.

THINGS TO AVOID

1. Do not dip the Flag of the United States to any person or any thing. The regimental color, State flag, organization or institutional flag will render this honor. At sea the Flag may be dipped in acknowledgment of the salute of the flag of another nation.

2. Do not display the Flag of the United States with the union down, except as a signal of distress.

3. Do not place any other flag or pennant above or to the right of the Flag of the United States.

4. Do not let the Flag of the United States touch the ground or trail in the water.

5. Do not place any object or emblem of any kind on or above the Flag of the United States.

6. Do not use the Flag as drapery; use bunting.

7. Do not fasten the Flag in such manner as will permit it to be easily torn.

8. Do not drape the Flag over the hood, top or sides of a vehicle, or of a railroad train or boat. If it is desired to display the Flag on a motor car affix the staff firmly to the chassis or clamp it to the radiator cap.

9. Do not use the Flag to cover a speaker's desk or to drape over front of a platform or over chairs or benches.

10. Do not display the Flag on a float in a parade except on a staff.

11. Do not use the Flag as a ceiling covering.

12. Do not use the Flag of the United States as a portion of costume or of an athletic uniform. Do not embroider it upon cushions or handkerchiefs or print it on paper napkins or boxes.

13. Do not put lettering upon the Flag.

14. Do not use the Flag of the United States in any form of advertising nor fasten an advertising sign to a flag-pole.

15. Do not display, use or store the Flag in such a manner as will permit it to be easily soiled or damaged.

PROPER USE OF BUNTING

Bunting of the national colors should be used for covering speakers' desks, draping over front of platforms and for decoration in general. Bunting should be arranged with the blue above, the white in the middle and the red below.

SALUTE TO THE FLAG

During the ceremony of hoisting or lowering the Flag or when the Flag is passing in parade or review all persons present should stand at attention facing the Flag. Men's headdress should be removed with the right hand and held at the left shoulder. Those present in uniform should salute with the right hand. Women should stand at attention facing the Flag or as the Flag is passing in parade should salute by placing the right hand over the heart. If the national anthem is played and no flag is present all stand at attention when uncovered and salute at the first note of the anthem, retaining the position until the last note of the air is played. If in civilian dress and covered men should uncover and stand at attention facing the music.

PLEDGE TO THE FLAG

I pledge allegiance to the Flag of the United States and the Republic for which it stands, one nation indivisible, with liberty and justice for all.

THE SHIELD OF THE UNITED STATES

The shield of the United States has thirteen vertical stripes, seven white and six red with a blue chief without stars.

NATIONAL ANTHEM

The Star-Spangled Banner is recommended for universal recognition as the national anthem.

FEDERAL FLAG LAWS

There is but one Federal statute which protects the Flag throughout the country from desecration. This law provides that a trademark cannot be registered which consists of or comprises, among other things, the Flag, coat of arms or other insignia of the United States or any simulation thereof. (33 Stat. L. p. 725, Feb. 20, 1905.)

Congress has also enacted legislation providing certain penalties for the desecration, mutilation or improper use of the Flag within the District of Columbia. (Feb. 8, 1917, 39 Stat. L. page 900.)

SUGGESTIONS FOR STATE LEGISLATION

Based upon opinion of the Supreme Court of the United States, rendered by Justice John Marshall Harlan, every State should enact adequate laws for the protection of the national flag. State flag laws should include the following:

1. That June 14, Flag Day, be set apart by proclamation of the Governor, recommending that Flag Day be observed by people generally by the display of the Flag of the United States and in such other ways as will be in harmony with the general character of the day.

2. That the Flag of the United States be displayed on the main administration buildings of each public institution.

3. That the Flag of the United States with staff or flag pole be provided each schoolhouse and be displayed during schooldays either from a flag-staff or in inclement weather within the school building.

4. That the Flag of the United States be displayed in every polling place.

5. That the use of the Flag of the United States as a receptacle for receiving, holding, carrying or delivering anything be prohibited.

6. That the use of the Flag for advertising purposes in any manner be prohibited.

7. That penalty (fine and imprisonment) be provided for public mutilation, abuse or desecration of the Flag.

INDEX